he

www. **Tameside** .gov.uk

speech

# how to write
## a wedding
# speech

hamlyn

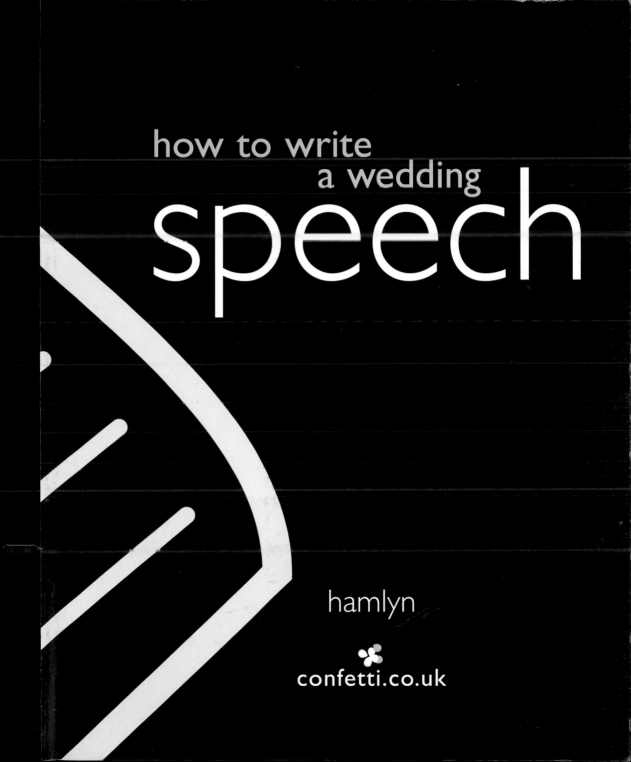

confetti.co.uk

First published in Great Britain in 2007 by
Hamlyn, a division of Octopus Publishing Group Ltd
2–4 Heron Quays, London E14 4JP

ISBN-13: 978-0-600-61644-3
ISBN-10: 0-600-61644-4

A CIP catalogue record for this book is available from
the British Library

Printed and bound in China

10 9 8 7 6 5 4 3 2 1

# contents

Introduction 6

Planning your speech 8

Winning lines and toasts 44

The father of the bride's speech 56

The groom's speech 76

The best man's speech 96

The bride's speech 114

The chief bridesmaid's speech 128

Standing in 138

Civil partnerships 150

Index 158

About confetti.co.uk 160

# Introduction

Let's be honest here: there are three things that most guests remember about a wedding. What the bride wore; how long they had to wait before eating; and how good the speeches were.

If the last item on that list fills you with dread, then chances are you're lined up to speak at your own wedding, or that of a daughter, son or friend. Never fear, this book is here to help.

Before you get too stressed at the prospect, put your speech into perspective. True, you'll be the centre of attention for five minutes or so, but the day really belongs to the couple, and most of the time everyone will be focusing on them. The trick is to make your five minutes really count.

Of course, you will need to add your own personal touches, anecdotes and asides. But we hope the following will give you lots of ideas.

## Who is this book for?

In a nutshell: this book is for anybody and everybody who is going to make a speech at a wedding or civil ceremony.

Few people find it easy to speak in public. In fact, in one recent poll respondents rated public speaking as more stressful than moving house or going through a divorce.

Try to relax. Speakers at weddings aren't chosen for their legendary oratorical skills. The guests won't mind if you're not Woody Allen or Bill Clinton. What they want to hear are warm, affectionate, gently humorous words about their loved ones.

Sure, you're going to be nervous. But (a) guests expect you to be, and will forgive you and (b) there are things you can do to calm down (see pages 34–37). It may be a cliché but it really is true: *everyone is on your side.*

And so is this book. Inside you'll find all kinds of useful stuff on what to say, what not to say, how to say it and when. Above all, you'll find loads of material that you can tweak and make your own.

The first chapter is packed with ideas for putting together a great speech – research, subject matter, props, games and more. The second chapter gives you lots of material for toasts, one-liners, jokes and ice-breakers.

Chapters 3–7 focus on the different speakers: father of the bride, groom, best man, bride, chief bridesmaid. And in the eighth chapter, we offer some help for one of the trickiest roles of all: the stand-in speaker. The last chapter discusses speaking at a civil partnership ceremony.

Throughout you'll find plenty of sample content to help you craft your own winning words.

For more ideas and resources, why not visit our website (www.confetti.co.uk). There you will find expert advice to help you with every aspect of your speech.

So good luck. You're going to be fine – in fact, you may find you even enjoy yourself. Now get out there and knock their socks off!

# Planning
## your speech

# Who are you and what should you say?

## Who speaks and when

Traditionally, the toastmaster or master of ceremonies will introduce the speeches at the end of the meal. The formal order of speakers is:

- Father of the bride (or a close family friend)
- The groom
- The best man

The bride, chief bridesmaid or other guests may want to speak, too. If so, they will usually speak before the best man.

Traditionally, the speeches take place after the meal, but some couples decide to have them beforehand to allow the speakers to enjoy their meal free of nerves.

## Who says what?

Here is a brief outline of who says what. For more details and for sample speech snippets, turn to the relevant chapters.

### Father of the bride or friend of the family

- Thanks the guests for coming and participating in the special day.
- Thanks everyone who has contributed to the cost of the wedding.
- Compliments and praises the bride, and welcomes her new husband into the family.
- Toasts the bride and groom.

### Bridegroom

- Thanks the father of the bride for his toast.
- Thanks the guests for attending and for their gifts.
- Thanks both sets of parents.
- Compliments his bride.
- Thanks his best man.
- Thanks and toasts the bridesmaids.

### Best man

- Thanks the groom for his toast to the bridesmaids.
- Comments on the bridal couple, particularly the groom.
- Reads out any messages from absent friends and relatives.
- Toasts the bride and groom.

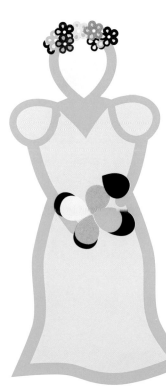

### Bride

- Reiterates the thanks already given – especially for the gifts.
- Thanks anyone who has not already been thanked by the speakers or may not be mentioned by them.
- Compliments her groom.

### Chief bridesmaid

- Compliments the bride and thanks her for choosing her.
- Compliments the ushers on behalf of the bridesmaids.
- Toasts the bride and groom.

# Cardinal rules

Unaccustomed as you are, you're scheduled for a spot of speech-making. Stick to the cardinal rules and make your piece a sure-fire success.

### Pick the right tone

Tone can be tricky. In making your speech, you have to fulfil certain obligations.

- You need to express thanks and convey affection and sincerity. You want to avoid coming across as too serious, dull or even pompous.
- You should aim to entertain. A speech without humour is a boring thing indeed, but a speech that sounds like a second-rate stand-up comedian on an off-night can be impersonal and lacking in warmth. Be funny, but never risk giving offence.
- The ideal tone is one of gentle humour, intimacy and affection. Try to aim for something that makes everyone feel included.

## Keep it short

However fabulous your wedding speech, the golden rule is always to leave your audience wanting more. Your performance should, as Oscar Wilde once said, 'be exquisite, and leave one unsatisfied.'

- Wedding guests enjoy speeches, but don't overestimate their boredom threshold. However funny you are, if you go on for too long, noisy coughing fits are sure to set in. With speeches, less is always more and brevity really is the soul of wit.
- Stick to quick-fire quips rather than shaggy-dog stories; anecdotes rather than sagas; pithy comments rather than rambling digressions.
- To help you get it right, time yourself when you practise.

## Don't wing it

Take time to prepare and write your speech. You don't have to scribble everything down at once.

- Keep your speech in the back of your mind for a few weeks before the wedding and jot down ideas as they occur to you.
- Ask others for anecdotes and use books and quotations, as well as your imagination, to help you create your masterpiece.
- Hone your performance by rehearsing, preferably with people you can rely on for honest, constructive feedback.

# Cardinal sins

Wedding speeches should be memorable. But make sure guests remember your speech for the right reasons – not the fact that you mentioned the bride's three previous husbands, for example. Here's what NOT to do.

## Don't mention the war...

Keep in mind that you will probably have a very mixed audience. Aim to make your speech appeal to everyone and, most importantly, avoid anything that may cause offence.

- You have to include all the guests – for example, not everyone will know that Mr Trimble was your woodwork teacher. If an anecdote can't easily be explained, leave it out.
- Swearing is a definite no-go area. The last thing you need is granny fainting at a four-letter word.
- Bear in mind that causing offence in a wedding speech could be preserved forever on video, in the minds of the guests and the couple!
- Finally, whatever feelings you may have about the couple's compatibility, this is not the time to let your hostility show. If you can't make a positive speech, delegate to someone who can.

## Don't ramble

Being asked to speak at a wedding is a compliment, so plan what you are going to say properly. You need to know where you are going with your speech.

- Create a definite structure with a beginning, middle and end.
- Long, rambling speeches are likely to send the older guests off to sleep, so keep it short.
- Likewise, long drawn-out jokes may fall flat if they take too long to tell – spare a thought for guests' memory lapses.

## Don't mumble

The cardinal sins here are swallowing your words, speaking too fast and losing your place (in which case you might as well admit it and get a laugh). This is one of the few times in life when you can be guaranteed a captive and sympathetic audience. They want to make life easy for you, so help them.

- As soon as you start your speech, check that everyone in the room can hear you.
- Speak slowly and clearly.
- Signal jokes by pausing to allow everyone to laugh!

# Good preparation

**What kind of speech to make**

Decide what kind of speech you want to make before you start putting it together. You could:

- Make a speech on your own.
- Make a joint speech.
- Perform a stunt and/or use props.
- Use a home video or slides or invent funny telegrams.
- Adopt a well-known format to comic effect.

## Preparing your speech

Preparation is at the heart of a good speech. Scribbling down a few words the night before the big day is not going to work. You may start formulating some ideas as soon as you know you are going to give a speech, but keep them on the back burner and really start working on it a few weeks before the wedding.

It's an unfailing rule: the more prepared you are, the more confident you will be about giving your speech, and the more your audience will enjoy it. And the more you'll enjoy the experience, too.

## Break down each element

Don't think about your speech as one big lump. Break it down into headings and decide what you're going to say under each one. For instance, if you are the best man – how you met the groom, the wedding preparations, or how the bride and groom got to know each other. Then look at all the elements and work out the best order in which to fit them together.

### Speech-making aids

As you prepare, make sure you have:

- A notebook so you can jot down ideas as they occur to you.
- A tape recorder so you can practise and time your speech.
- Asked friends and family to listen to your speech and give you ideas.
- Decided what props (if any) you are using and how to use them.
- A copy of the latest draft of your speech to carry round with you, so you can make notes and work on it whenever you want.

# Do your research

While most speakers at a wedding will simply be required to say a few kind words and possibly make a toast, it is usually the best man's speech that is most eagerly anticipated by guests – he is generally expected to liven up the proceedings by being witty and entertaining! The tips given in the rest of this chapter will help anyone who is making a wedding speech and will be particularly useful for all those who are going to act as best man.

Good research can turn a mildly amusing speech into an uproariously funny one. Nothing can beat that cringe-inducing anecdote or photo from the couple's early years that the father of the bride or best man has managed to excavate and that they were clearly hoping no one could possibly remember – and may even have forgotten about themselves.

People love hearing stories about the bride and groom's family life or early schooldays, so give them what they want. Start your research early to gather everything you need.

## Friends united

The best sources of stories about a bride and groom are, of course, their friends and family. Siblings, cousins, mates and colleagues probably all have some interesting anecdotes to tell. As soon as you know you're doing a speech, send out e-mails asking people who know the happy couple for any funny/touching stories they think you could include. Or invite everyone out for a drink, bring your tape recorder along and let them reminisce away. You're sure to come away with some great material.

## Every picture tells a story

Photograph albums are a rich source of speech material, too. Old pictures, or the stories behind them, can be hilarious. For instance, if there's a snap of the groom or bride pulling a face in a school photo or looking cute as a toddler, the best man could get it blown up to display on the night and work it into his speech.

A picture of the groom as a five-year-old enjoying a donkey ride at the seaside can be used as an illustration of his lifelong affection for the gee-gees, while a snap of him as a naked tot in the bath can show how much he's always loved water sports.

Not everyone at the wedding will have known the bride and groom for long. Using photographs of them as tiny children can help to bridge the gap between friends and family. It also gives licence to comment on their childhood hobbies, eccentricities and fashion sense, and make comical comparisons with the grown-up people they are today.

## What the papers say

Are there any newspaper cuttings about the happy couple? Perhaps he appeared in the local paper in his days as top goal scorer for the under-tens football team, or she was a prize-winning Girl Guide. This type of material can be used to illustrate how much they've changed... or how much they haven't, as the case may be.

News from the year the bride/groom were born can readily be worked into a speech. For example:

'1969 was the year Neil Armstrong took a small step for man and a giant leap for mankind by walking on the moon, and coincidentally, it was also the year Paul took his first steps...'

Computers can be used to great effect to create front page newspaper mock-ups: you could use a *Sun* headline such as 'Gotcha' to accompany a picture of the couple getting engaged. Get the picture blown up as large as possible and display it while you're making your speech.

## Written in the stars

Zodiac signs make for great speech fodder. Use them to compare the characteristics/vices of the sign the bride/groom were born under to the way that they actually are. If, for example, the groom's star sign says that he's generous and brave, but in fact he's notoriously thrifty and a bit of a coward, you're well away.

'Geminis are meant to be communicative and witty, with a reputation for being the life and soul of the party. Well, I guess that's one way of describing James on his stag night...'

Or:

'Helen's such a quiet, gentle girl that many people don't realize she's a Leo, which is, of course, a fire sign. But I can assure you that, as far as Richard is concerned, she's burning up with passion.'

Books that discuss star sign compatibility can also provide some funny lines for speeches, and so can reading out the horoscope for the day. It doesn't need to be a real one – just make up something to suit the occasion, for example, 'My horoscope says today is a day for pure relaxation – wonder what went wrong there then?'

## Stars in their eyes

Comparing the bride or groom to a celebrity or star with the same name, can work well in a speech. For example:

'Tom Cruise may have made his millions and worked with most of Hollywood's major directors, while our Tom has made a few quid and enjoys a pint of Directors. However, I think he's the more fortunate guy, as Tom Cruise didn't have much luck with Nicole, but Tom has got Isabel, and their love is something money and fame can't buy.'

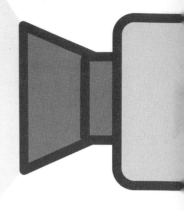

## Whatever they like...

Hobbies and interests of all kinds can form the basis of lots of stories. However, you might not be as familiar with the groom's obsessions as he is. In this case, the Internet is a great source of information.

   If one of the happy couple is a huge fan of any singer or celebrity and their obsession is well known, you could use it in your speech. For example:

'Roger has always been a major Elvis fan, and when he met Rachel he was certainly All Shook Up. He almost moved into Heartbreak Hotel when he thought she wasn't interested...'

## Make it work

Working life and old bosses can be a source of great material. If you're not a colleague of the bride or groom, get in touch with their workmates past and present and ask them for any good office anecdotes. Just make sure that everyone will understand them.

## Ha ha ha

Jokes, jokes, jokes – everyone likes to hear them at weddings. As well as your own jokes, renting comedy videos and films, asking people for their favourite gags and looking for funny lines on the Internet can also provide you with inspiration.

   If you do borrow jokes, you will need to personalize them to make them appropriate, rather than just throw them into a speech. The following sections of this book are full of examples of how to do this. Go for quality rather than quantity: a handful of well-polished witticisms will do you better service than a hundred ill-digested one-liners.

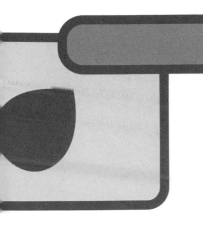

## By any other name...

There's often mileage in the meaning of the names of the bride or groom:

*'Apparently, the name Gary means "spear carrier". Well, I don't know about a spear but he certainly carries a torch for Kathleen.'*

You could also compare the meanings of the couple's names.

## Academic archive

Old schoolbooks, school reports and university notes can also provide material. Ask the bride or groom's family to get them down from the attic and take a look. If there's a school report saying how your high-flying friend will never amount to a hill of beans, or a funny essay they wrote when they were ten, it could be amusing to read it out.

### Get some help

If you're worried about any aspect of your speech, talk it through with someone who's been there before.

Talking to someone with experience will calm your nerves and give your confidence a boost. They survived the ordeal, after all! And if they still have a copy of their speech, ask to see it. They can also advise on how to source material, where they got their ideas from and how they put the whole thing together.

You can also learn from their mistakes. They may have unwittingly stumbled on a sensitive subject, for example, or their speech may have overrun or been too short. Ask them which parts really worked, and what were the things that could, in retrospect, have been improved on. Finding out how not to do it can be a great help. And if they are willing, ask them to read your speech after you've written it, for some last-minute expert advice.

# The right material

Wedding speakers have it tough. Who else has to make a speech that will appeal to an audience with an age range of 2 to 82? Speeches have to make people laugh without offending anyone's sensibilities, talk about families and relationships without treading on anyone's toes and hold people's attention.

## Tips for success

It sounds like a tall order, but most of the pitfalls of speech-making can be avoided if you know what to talk about and recognize that there are limits around certain subjects. It's all a matter of choosing and using your material with care.

- **Criticism** Weddings aren't the place for criticism. Don't knock anything relating to the venue or the service. Don't make jokes at other people's expense, especially the bride's. This is the happy couple's perfect day, and you need to help keep it that way by considering other people's feelings at all times.

- **The bride** It's possible that you may have ambivalent feelings about the bride. Keep these firmly under wraps at the wedding. Don't make any jokey remarks about her diet either! Compliments to

the bride are the only permissible references to her in your speech.

- **Be kind** Remember, if you're opting for a funny speech to mix the mockery with some sincerity. Talk about how highly you think of both the bride and groom and how their relationship together has enriched each other. Give the couple all your very best wishes for the future.

- **Include everyone** To make sure no one feels left out, imagine all the different types of people who might be listening to your speech and try to include something for everyone. Avoid in-jokes and make sure you explain references to people and places some listeners may not be familiar with. Be sensitive about the sensibilities of all the guests: that stag night 'moonie' may not amuse everyone!

## Quick speech checklist

- Does your speech fit the occasion? Is it light-hearted and positive?
- Have you tested it on other people and asked for their honest feedback?
- Have you timed it to ensure it's not too long?
- Have you been careful not to offend anyone? Or leave anyone out?
- Do you know in what order the speeches will be made and at what time?
- If there is a microphone, do you know how to use it?
- Have you written notes, in case you dry up?
- Have you checked names and how to pronounce them?
- Have you made a note of everyone you need to thank, or any messages to be read out?

## Tailored to fit

The material that you decide is suitable for your speech will depend on your audience. It's up to you to find out who you'll be talking to, and to check beforehand that what you want to say won't cause offence. If you can rehearse your speech in front of your mum and granny without them feeling uncomfortable or you feeling embarrassed, you're probably on to a winner.

# The do's and don'ts of good subject matter

| Subject | What's expected | Do say | Don't say |
| --- | --- | --- | --- |
| The happy couple's relationship | Comments about the bride and groom are usually part of every wedding speech. Tread carefully, however, especially if their relationship has been stormy in the past. | Tell guests about how their first meeting generated enough electricity to power the National Grid. Talk about how compatible they are and how great they both look today. | Don't tell them about how they slept together within half-an-hour of meeting or about how she left him for someone else for six months. Arguments, estrangements and threats to call off the wedding are all off limits. If in any doubt, leave it out. |
| Bit of a lad | People expect funny stories about the groom's misconducts, especially when part of the best man's speech. Joshing him gently is all part of the fun, but do make sure that your anecdotes are humorous rather than offensive. | Tell guests about the time he redecorated the living room with crayons when he was a little lad. | Don't tell them about how he was all over that lap dancer at his stag night, then vomited copiously in the minicab all the way home. Keep quiet about criminal records, expulsions from school and the like, too. |

| Subject | What's expected | Do say | Don't say |
|---|---|---|---|
| Family matters | Complimenting the bride and groom's families can be part of your speech – but make sure you stick to compliments only. | Tell guests how the bride/groom have great parents – and now they're gaining great parents-in-law, as well as a lovely wife/husband. Or congratulate the parents for organizing the wedding so well. | Don't tell them how you're amazed to see the bride/groom's father there at all since he walked out when the groom was still in his pram. Speeches shouldn't be used for settling scores. Avoid comments about divorced or warring parents. If the family situation is very sensitive, resist the temptation to think you can make things better with a few carefully chosen lines. |
| The wedding | Behind-the-scenes stories about preparing for the wedding, especially amusing incidents and narrowly averted disasters, make good ingredients for speeches. However, you might be surprised at how sensitive these subjects can be. Very few families don't have a couple of squabbles over wedding arrangements. These disagreements often seem amusing by the time the big day arrives, but sometimes they don't – so take care. | Tell guests how fantastically the day has turned out and how it's all down to the hard work of all the organizers. | Don't tell them about how the bride's mother almost had a nervous breakdown over the seating plan – unless you're absolutely sure she'll think it's funny. As always, run your speech by someone close to the family first. |

| Subject | What's expected | Do say | Don't say |
|---|---|---|---|
| In-jokes | Making everyone feel included is an important job of any speaker. To make sure no one feels left out, think of all the people who might be listening when you write your speech. You need to explain references that not everyone may be familiar with, and if this takes too long, it's better to think of another anecdote. | Tell guests about how, one year, the bride/groom broke three dozen eggs in the school egg and spoon race. | Don't tell them about that hilarious time in design and technology class when the bride/groom got told off by Mr Smith, you know, the technology teacher who was really mad, and he sent her/him to see Miss Green, the one who all the lads fancied... you really had to be there. |

# Using props

Physical gags, games, visuals and tricks can all be part of a good speech. So if you don't want to just read a prepared text, let your imagination run wild. If your speech is going to involve the use of props, make sure that you do plenty of rehearsing with them beforehand, and also ensure that any machinery is in good working order before the big day.

## Five great prop ideas

### I Make 'em look

Simple props can be used to begin with a bang. One best man, for instance, started off his speech with the remark: 'I hate it when people use cheap gimmicks to get attention, don't you?' before whipping off his baseball cap and ponytail to reveal a completely bald pate.

Lots of different props can be used for this type of joke. Why not try:

- A revolving bow tie
- A whistle
- A clown nose?

### 2 Read the signs

Introduce your speech by saying that you've got a sore throat and can't speak very loudly, so your friend is going to use sign language to interpret what you're saying. Your friend will then make exaggerated and ridiculous hand gestures to accompany your speech. Obviously, this one will need a lot of rehearsal.

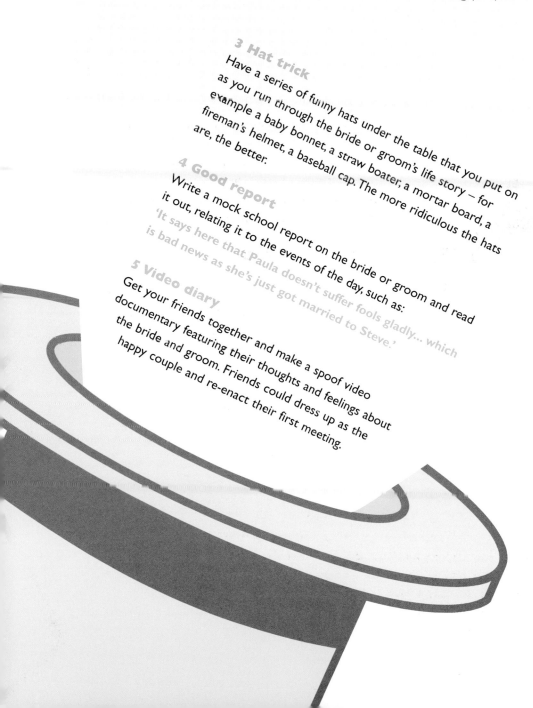

### 3 Hat trick

Have a series of funny hats under the table that you put on as you run through the bride or groom's life story – for example a baby bonnet, a straw boater, a mortar board, a fireman's helmet, a baseball cap. The more ridiculous the hats are, the better.

### 4 Good report

Write a mock school report on the bride or groom and read it out, relating it to the events of the day, such as:

'It says here that Paula doesn't suffer fools gladly... which is bad news as she's just got married to Steve.'

### 5 Video diary

Get your friends together and make a spoof video documentary featuring their thoughts and feelings about the bride and groom. Friends could dress up as the happy couple and re-enact their first meeting.

# Fun games to play

Playing speech games is a way of getting the whole audience to join in the fun. Try the following:

## The singing game

Ask friends and family to help compile a list of words that describe the guests at each table. Put the lists on the respective tables and ask everyone sitting at them to make up a song or poem using all of the words on the list. They then have to stand up and perform it!

## The limerick game

This is another word game that everyone can enjoy. You put a note on all the tables asking the guests to make up a short poem or limerick about the couple. You can read out the best ones during your speech, or ask the guests to read out their own. Make it clear however, that you don't want anything offensive.

## The sweepstake game

At the start of the reception, get the ushers to ask guests to bet on the length of the speeches. The person who makes the closest guess wins the total amount, either to keep or to donate to a charity of their choice.

## The key game

This is a favourite for best man speeches as it really helps to break the ice. To play it, you need to have a word with all the female guests beforehand (you might have to hang around the ladies at the reception to do it) and fill them in on the plan.

During your speech you say something like:

'Neil has got what you might call a chequered past, but now that he's married to Hannah it's time that he began afresh. So I'm asking any of his ex-girlfriends who may be present to give back the keys to his flat. Just come up here and put them in this bowl. Come on girls, don't be shy.'

Then, you've guessed it, all the women at the reception, from the groom's 90-year-old auntie to his four-year-old cousin will come up to put a set of keys in the bowl. It's guaranteed to get laughs and helps everyone to relax.

# Good delivery

## It ain't what you do...

As anyone who's made a successful speech will tell you, it's not what you say, it's the way you say it. And, you want to make sure the way you deliver and present your speech does justice to your carefully written masterpiece. Here's how.

## Practice makes perfect

Reading your speech out again and again before the big day is essential if you want to perfect your delivery, ensure your material is suitable and find out if your jokes are really funny. Your speech should appeal to everyone, from your friends to your maiden aunt, so try to rehearse in front of a variety of people.

Test it out on people who will give honest, constructive feedback. They will also be able to tell you when you're mumbling, or rambling, or just going on too long.

You should also record your rehearsals on tape. That way, you will be able to review yourself and see where there's room for improvement and how you are for time – aim for five minutes as a rough guide.

## The run-up

You've enjoyed a tearful moment during the wedding ceremony and the celebrations and reception have begun. Good food and wine is flowing but all you can think about is how nervous you are about your imminent speech. How you fill your time will affect your delivery.

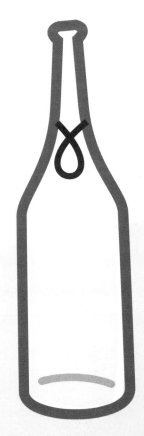

## Don't overindulge

Although it's very tempting to
down a few too many glasses while
you're waiting to speak – don't. Being
tipsy could affect your delivery by making you
slur your words and cause you to be unsteady on
your feet. Too many drinks might also lead you to decide that
the risqué story which you deleted from your original
speech, really should be in there after all.

## Have a banana

Many professional performers swear by the trick of eating a
banana about 20 minutes before they start speaking. Doing
this, they say, will give you a quick energy boost and help
steady your nerves.

# Useful prompts

## Memory joggers

Reading an entire speech from a sheet of paper can make it sound a bit lifeless and can stop you from making eye contact with the audience. One of the ways to get around this is to memorize your speech and use prompts to remind you of what to say.

To cut down on the amount of text you use, first write the speech out, then make very brief notes that remind you of each part of it. Gradually cut back on your text, so the notes say as much as you need to jog your memory.

## On cue

Make a set of cue cards. These are small index cards with key phrases that remind you of different parts of your speech, stacked in the order that you say them. Inserting blank cards for pauses can help you pace your speech. Even if you feel you need to put your whole speech on cards, they are still preferable to a piece of paper, because you will need to pause and look up as you turn them.

## What the experts say

'The more you practise delivering your speech, the less nervous you will be. Practise the pauses, the intonations, the anecdotes. By showing you've put even a little thought and effort into what you're saying, all manner of sins will be forgiven. Recite your speech in the shower. On the bus. On the loo. On the night, your nerves will thank you, because instead of fretting about the audience or your flies, you'll simply focus on what you're going to say.'
*Ruh Pointer, stand-up comic and serial best man*

'Don't speak when you're looking down at your notes. Look down for a moment, look up, smile at everyone, speak – then repeat. You don't need to talk constantly; it gives guests a break, and if you're not afraid of silence, you'll look confident, so everyone can relax. Remember that in between speaking silence feels approximately ten times longer than it is, so take it nice and slow.'
*Jill Edwards, comedy coach and scriptwriter*

# Ten steps to success

Timing is crucial when it comes to speeches. However brilliant yours is, and however good a speaker you are, five minutes is more than enough. People enjoy listening to speeches, but they also want to get on with talking and dancing, so keep it short. Make sure yours has a firm beginning, middle and end. Steer clear of rambling stories in favour of short, pithy jokes and asides. When it comes to speeches, less is definitely more.

Don't try to begin your speech when there are lots of distractions. Wait until the audience has settled down, stopped applauding the previous speaker and you have people's undivided attention.

## 1  Make eye contact

Make eye contact when you're making your speech – just not with everyone at once! Speak as if you were talking to one person and focus on them. You can look around the room if you want to, but focus on one person at a time. The trick is to imagine that you're simply chatting to someone.

## 2  Don't look down

Even if you decide to learn your speech off by heart, you will need to have some notes to refer to in case your mind goes blank in the heat of the moment. However, don't deliver your speech while hiding behind a quivering piece of paper or constantly staring downwards. Look down for a moment, look up and speak. Get into a rhythm of doing this throughout your speech.

### 3  Breathe properly

When people get nervous, they tend to swallow their words; this can render a beautifully written speech nearly inaudible. You don't want to deliver your speech only to find that no one could actually hear what you were saying. An effective way to combat the mumbling menace is by breathing properly – take deep, rhythmic breaths, as this will pump oxygen into your blood and keep your brain sharp and alert. Check that you're audible by arranging beforehand for someone at the back of the room to signal when your voice isn't carrying.

### 4  Set a good pace

Gabbling is another thing people tend to do when they're nervous. To stop yourself talking too fast, write the word 'pause' at intervals through your notes, or if you are using cue cards, insert blank ones that will automatically cause you to slow down. If you do lose your place, it's best just to make a joke of it.

### 5  Time your jokes

Pause briefly after you make a joke to give people a chance to laugh, but keep jokes and anecdotes short so that if one doesn't work, you can move on quickly to the next. If your joke dies, don't despair. Turn the situation to your advantage by inserting a quip such as 'Only me on that one then', or look round at an imaginary assistant and say: 'Start the car!' 'Rescue lines' like these can earn you a chuckle from a momentarily awkward silence.

## 6  Remember to smile

Making a speech is supposed to be fun, so make sure you don't look utterly miserable when you're doing it. Smile! Think of something that makes you laugh before you start speaking to get yourself in the right mood. Body language is important, too, so adopt a relaxed posture before you begin – no crossed arms or fidgeting.

## 7  Start strongly

Opening lines are important, because they grab the audience's attention and get you off to a good start. Something like: 'Ladies and gentlemen, they say speeches are meant to be short and sweet, so thank you and good night,' should help you to begin in style.

## 8  Think positively

Instead of seeing your speech as a formal ordeal, think of it as being a conversation between you and a lot of people you know and really like, or as a way of wishing two good friends well. Thinking positively about your speech and the reason why you are there will help you to deliver it with confidence and make the task seem less intimidating.

Remember that weddings are happy occasions and all the guests want to see everything go well, including your speech. Be assured, the audience is on your side, they're all rooting for you, so make the most of it and use their goodwill to boost your confidence.

To help calm your nerves, imagine your speech being over and everyone applauding. Imagine how you'll feel when you can sit down, relax and really enjoy the rest of the evening. By visualizing everything going well, you should gain even more confidence.

## 9 Convey your message

Think about the meaning of your speech while you're making it. Concentrate on the thoughts you want to convey and the message behind your words, rather than just reciting your notes, as this will help you to make your delivery much more expressive.

## 10 End with a toast

End your speech with a toast. This will give it a focus and provide something to work towards. After you make your toast, you can sit down when everyone else sits down, signifying a definite end to your speech.

### Stage fright
It's only natural to be nervous. If you find that you're really scared when you begin, don't panic. Make a joke out of it instead. Lines like 'This speech is brought to you in association with Imodium' or 'I was intending to speak but my tongue seems to be welded to the roof of my mouth' should raise a laugh and will help to get the audience on your side. One completely bald father of the bride started off on a high note by remarking: 'As you can see, I've been so worried about making this speech, I've been tearing my hair out.' There's no shame in admitting you're a wee bit scared.

# Wedding speech checklist

### Once you've agreed to speak

- Start thinking about research.
- Think about the audience. Your speech will have to appeal to a wide range of people.
- It's your job to find out who'll be among the guests so that your material appeals and you don't cause offence.
- Ask friends and family for funny stories/embarrassing pictures that you can build into your speech.
- Keep your speech in the back of your mind. You never know when you might pick up a some juicy material.
- Keep a notebook to hand to jot down ideas.
- Speak to someone who's been a wedding speaker before and find out what not to do.

- Decide on the kind of speech you want. Will you need any props or visual aids or any equipment?

### The build-up

- Think about the structure. Would the speech be better broken down into manageable chunks/themes?
- Does your speech do what it's supposed to do? Is it funny, affectionate and charming without being offensive?
- Have you included everything you need to say in your speech?
- Gather all the props/presentation aids you'll need and make sure you know how to use them.
- Build in time to practise your speech – the better rehearsed you are, the more confident you'll be, and the more everyone will enjoy it, yourself included.

## Only a week to go

- Use a tape recorder or video to record yourself.
- Rope in an audience of friends to practise on.
- Be sure to practise your speech with any props you plan to use – winging it on the day is not a good bet.
- Time your speech. Aim to keep it to around five minutes.
- Don't forget to allow time for reading out messages from absent friends and family.

- Write your speech in note form on cue cards, even if you intend to commit it to memory.
- Think positively about your speech and it will feel like less of an ordeal.
- Visualize your speech being over and everyone applauding as it will help to give you confidence and calm your nerves.
- Remember the audience is on your side – you'll be able to use their goodwill to boost your confidence.

## The big day

A few last pointers to help your speech go smoothly:

- Try to relax and take it easy.
- Try not to look for Dutch courage in the bottom of your wine glass – you'll do your speech more harm than good!
- Keep busy with your other duties; this will help you to focus, and keep away those pre-speech nerves.
- Have your notes with you, even if you've committed your speech to memory. If your mind goes blank or you feel yourself veering off the point, at least you can refer to them, to get back on track.
- End your speech with a toast – it will give you something to work towards and be a clear signal that your bit is over.

# Winning
# lines
## and toasts

# Structuring your speech

A good speech should have a strong start, a meaty middle and end on a high. That's why we've included this section that features a selection of beginnings, middles and endings. Read them through, choose the sections that appeal and copy them in order – and you will have a basic structure to work with.

## Good beginnings

### Opening gambits

If your speech doesn't have a good start, guests will glaze over until the champagne toast. Try these to get you going...

'Excuse me, but I'm a little nervous. Now I know what a Rowntree's jelly feels like.'

'They say good speeches are meant to be pithy, although what oranges have got to do with it, I don't know.'

'They say good speeches are meant to be short and sweet... So thanks very much for your time.'

## Starting off

Adopt a mock-solemn expression, then say as you make the sign of the cross:

'In the name of the father and the son and the... (pause, look confused) Oh no. Sorry. We've done that bit.'

'Brevity, as I explain on page 72 of my speech, is indeed the soul of wit.'

### One-liners

'The groom was not always as handsome as this. When he was born the midwife took one look and slapped his father. He had the only pram in Bristol with shutters. In fact, he was so ugly his mum used to feed him with a catapult.'

'Jon has a face that launched a thousand ships. And a figure that ate a thousand chips.'

'Greg was always considered a handsome chap at college. He was fastidious about getting his beauty sleep – about 20 hours a day, usually.'

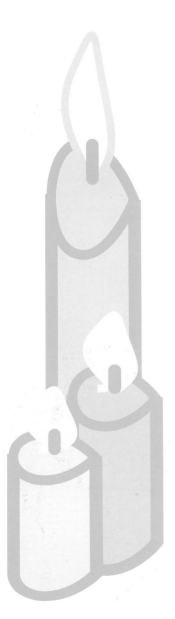

'Tony always used to take Janine out to dine in a secluded corner, lit only by candles. Partly because he's a romantic, but partly because he didn't want to scare her off!'

'Now he's married, Dom can really let himself go... oh, you already have!'

### Anecdotes

'The first time Bill and Emily went away together, Emily wanted Bill to act as if they were married, to avoid any disapproving looks. So Bill let her carry the suitcases.'

'Was it love at first sight the night Ian and Sue met? There are several theories about this. Sue contends that it was love at first sight, but then she found out he already had a boyfriend, so she went home with Ian instead...'

'These two eventually found each other after years of trying. And, as practice makes perfect, they really must be the perfect couple.'

'Rob and I have been great mates for a long time now, and inevitably we've shared many things over the years: our AA counsellor; our probation officer; our therapist; our mums' recipes for bread sauce – and now, a top table. Who'd have thought it?'

## Meaty middles

You should aim to add between three and six 'fillings' to your
speech sandwich.

### Something sentimental

'Every man hopes to find the perfect woman. In fact, a
lot of us spend most of our youth looking for her. Along
the way there may be a little bit of heartbreak. But
usually there is a lot of fun, too. I know that Andy has
had his fair share of heartache and more than his fair
share of fun. But now that he's with Suzanne, his search
is over. He's found the woman of his dreams. He's the
luckiest man alive and I couldn't be happier for him.'

'It's a real shame about the weather. I had such high hopes
that it was going to be a fine, sunny day today. I'm sure,
though, that the happy couple wouldn't have noticed if it was
snowing this afternoon. The two of them couldn't take their
eyes off each other. It does your heart good to see.'

### Religious references

'Thankfully our hosts, unlike those at the
wedding feast at Cana, haven't insisted on
saving the best wine till last! Though looking
at one or two of you here today, I'm not sure
you'd notice...'

'In the words of Saint Paul: "Forgive each other as soon
as a quarrel begins." Which is God's way of saying never go
to sleep on an argument...'

'As the Bible says: "Who so findeth a wife, findeth a good thing." Now when I look at Jane, I can't help thinking, what a complete understatement!'

'When God created man and woman in his own image, we're told he blessed them and said: "Be fruitful and multiply..." Now whatever did He mean by that?'

'Saint Paul advises us that "a husband must love his wife as he loves himself". Now if Jerry can pull THAT off, then Penny will be a really lucky gal...'

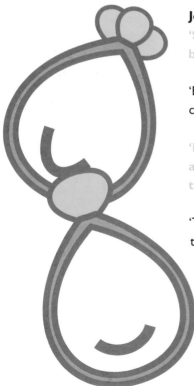

### Jokes and observations

'Sam and Sally are like very different wines: Sally gets better with age, whereas Sam just gets drunk.'

'Bob used to do 40 push-ups every morning to make sure he could keep up with Kirsty. Now he needs 40 winks...'

'Paula is busy making their new home comfortable, although Mark told me he's quite happy with his chair in the King's Head.'

'There are three kinds of wedding ring: the engagement ring, the wedding ring and the suffer-ring!'

'How many bridesmaids does it take to change a light bulb? Five. One to yank it out of the socket and chuck it, and four to squabble over who's going to catch it.'

'Some say that star-sign compatibility is the secret of a happy marriage. But I don't really believe in all that stuff – which is unusual for a Scorpio...'

'Some (single) people think that marriage will limit them or hold them back. But look at James and Katie today, and you see two people whose lives have expanded and flourished in every way since they got together...'

'My gran, who's been married 50 years, says the secret of a successful marriage is give and take. I said: "You mean 50:50"? She said: "NO! You've both got to give 110 per cent!"'

### Quips and asides

These are useful little remarks to allow you to comment on something topical or specific to the big day.

'Confucius, I believe, said something very significant about the meaning of marriage. But it was in Chinese, so I'm afraid I didn't understand it.'

"Thanks for giving me away Dad," Sally said to me this morning. "Think nothing of it," I replied. "I've been trying to do it for years!"'

'Given that Jemima and I have been living together for eight years, I thought that for once we deserved to walk up an aisle that's not located in Sainsbury's.'

'Before I continue, has anyone ever been to a wedding this posh before? Even the cockroaches have got place names...'

'Today was already shaping up to be a wonderful occasion – but look outside and you'll agree that, with gorgeous sunshine in mid-November, we've been truly blessed.'

(Note handed to speaker by usher)
'And before we go any further, some important news just in: Rochdale 4, Hartlepool 2.'

'By the way, please don't worry if you hear any unusual noises during the speeches – it's only Jim's wallet groaning in agony...'

'I must say I'm surprised by today's downpour. Sarah's parents have been such terrific wedding organizers, I assumed they'd be able to control the weather too!'

## End on a high

Nobody wants your speech to end. So leave them wanting more with something like...

'I'd like to thank you for your patience and kind attention, and to those of you who managed to stay awake: cheers!'

'That's all from me, except to say that, for those of you who've never given a speech at a wedding , if you get an audience half as generous as you lot, you'll enjoy every minute of it...'

'So, without further ado, I'd like you charge your glasses
and thank the Almighty that I'm finally going to sit
down and shut up. Cheers!'

'To the happy couple, may their happiness be complete, their
marriage long and prosperous and every wedding speech
they hear be funnier and shorter than mine...'

'And, in the words of that world-famous orator, Bugs
Bunny: "That's all, folks!"'

### Final thoughts

'One final thought. If marriage is a two-way street, how
come my wife keeps telling me that it's "my way or
the highway"?'

'One final thought. Always listen carefully to your partner's
advice, so that when things go wrong you can say, "I told
you so"!'

'And finally, marriage should be like supporting a
football team: sometimes happy, sometimes sad,
but always exciting for about an hour and a half on
a Saturday!'

'Don't forget. Never put off until tomorrow something
you can do today – especially if that something is saying,
"I love you".'

# Toasts

## What are toasts for?

Sincerity and practicality are the keys to a successful toast. A toast that comes from the heart will only add to the emotion of an already highly emotional day.

But toasts are of practical value, too. They can help punctuate a day that is always hectic and complicated by alerting guests to the end of speeches, and to the transition from one part of the wedding day to the next.

Toasts should have a clear purpose, whether it's simply to salute the bride and groom (usually the job of the best man) or to honour friends and family who couldn't make it and/or who have passed away.

Toasts can serve as a natural break in the proceedings if – as is often the case with the best man's speech – there have been a long list of thanks or other messages. And they're a quick and easy way to express additional thanks to specific members of the wedding party, such as the mothers of the bride and groom. If you are presenting gifts during a toast, for instance to the mothers or bridesmaids, make sure you leave time for the exchange to take place.

### The do's and don'ts of toast-making

Do instruct the guests as to what to do. For example: **'Please raise your glasses with me...' Give them time to do so before you launch into the actual toast.**

Do tell guests exactly what the wording of the toast is to be, for example 'To the bride and groom' or 'The happy couple!' Clarity is the key to a good toast.

Do keep your toast focused.

Do make your toast positive or funny.

Do finish your toast with a flourish and leave them wanting more.

Do sit when the guests sit down after the toast.

Don't rush into a toast before your guests have had time to follow your instructions, or it will end up confused and only half-heard.

Don't make your toast too complicated – or guests won't be able to follow it.

Don't forget, where appropriate, to include your partner in the toast if he/she isn't going to make a speech, for example: 'My wife and I would like to say a special thank you to the bridesmaids...'

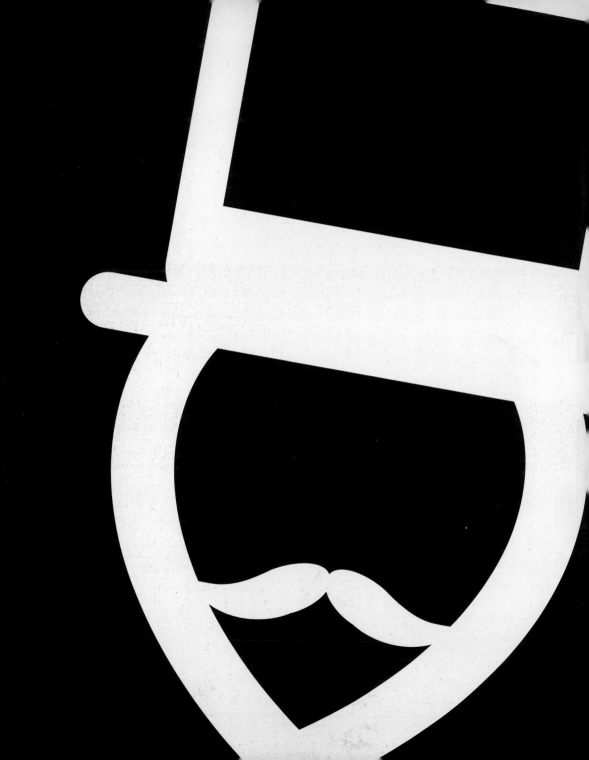

# The father
## of the bride's
# speech

# Father of the bride

Your daughter has chosen to marry, and it is your duty to send her into married life by celebrating her pre-wedding years in a sentimental – and possibly amusing – way. You've waited all your life for this moment, so take the time to enjoy it. This is your chance to tell her how much you care for her and let everyone else know how wonderful she is. Make the most of this opportunity.

## When you speak

Traditionally, the father of the bride is the first speaker (apart from a brief introduction from the best man), so your speech is a sort of scene-setter. The idea behind this is linked to the fact that the father of the bride was always supposed to foot the bill for the wedding – so if you're paying, you should at least be allowed to get your oar in first!

### What to say

- Thank anyone involved in planning (and paying for) the wedding.
- Speak proudly about your daughter and welcome the groom into your family.
- Thank everyone for coming.
- Propose a toast to the bride and groom.

### Alternatives

- Make a joint speech with your wife.
- Share the stage with a stepfather or godfather.
- Simply thank everyone for coming and propose a toast.
- Show a short film or candid camera shots of your daughter as a child.

# The basics

The father of the bride's speech is generally expected to be the least funny and often the most sentimental, which should make the job of writing it the easiest. But it's not always the case. This speech is often the one that has been anticipated for the longest period of time and is probably, if not the most emotional, then certainly the one filled with the most pride.

The father of the bride usually begins the speeches, thus setting the tone for the rest of the proceedings. The best advice is to stick largely with convention, unless you are feeling particularly brave or imaginative. It's easier to write a speech starting with the traditional component parts: welcoming the guests, thanking everyone, talking about the bride, welcoming the groom and, finally, making the toast.

**So what do you have to say?**
- Thank the guests for coming to the wedding and being involved in such a special day. Remember to mention anyone who has travelled a long distance.
- Thank anyone who has made some kind of financial contribution to the wedding.
- Tell your daughter how proud you are of her.
- Welcome your new son-in-law into your family.
- Reminisce about your daughter's pre-wedding years.
- Wish the newlyweds success and happiness in the future.
- Propose a toast to the bride and groom.

## Useful phrases

Here are various suggestions to consider incorporating into your wedding speech.

### 1 The welcome

- Thank you all for coming and sharing this special day with Nicola and John.
- I'd like to take this opportunity to thank you all for being here. I know that some of you have had further to come than others, but you are all welcome guests on this happy *day/night*.
- Ladies and gentlemen, I'm delighted to see so many of you here today to celebrate the marriage of my daughter Nicola to John.

### 2 The thanks

- Nicola and John have worked very hard to pay for today and it's been worth it. This is a lovely *meal/reception* and everything looks perfect. I'm proud of the pair of you.
- Weddings are not cheap occasions, but my *little girl/daughter* deserves the best and, as you can see, she's got it. This would not have been possible without the generous help of John's parents, George and Amy.
- This wedding has taken a lot of time and patience to organize, and decisions have sometimes been difficult to reach *(make a small joke about the struggle it was to decide between a sophisticated colour scheme or an outrageous one of pink with yellow spots)*, but I'm really delighted that everything's turned out so well. In particular, I'd like to thank the *florist/minister/bridesmaids* for the amount of trouble they have gone to. *Everything/the flowers/the church/the hall/the hotel* looks wonderful.

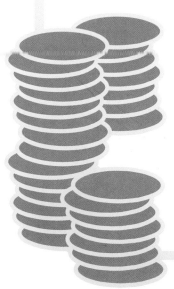

### 3  The bride

- I have always known that Nicola is a beautiful woman, but I have never seen her look quite so gorgeous or so radiant as she does today. I'm extremely proud of her.
- Nicola has had many roles in life... (for example, daughter, sister, student, lawyer), but never has she looked more lovely than as a bride.
- When Nicola told me that she was going to get married, I was worried that she wouldn't be my little girl any more, but seeing her today as a beautiful bride, I realize that no matter how old she is she will always be my baby and I love her.
- This *elegant/beautiful/radiant/lovely* bride is a far cry from the Nicola I remember so well, who was always in trouble for being *messy/muddy/late/a tomboy/scruffy*, but, no matter what she looks like I love her and am very proud to be her father.

If you're not the bride's father, there are many ways to convey how proud you are to take on this role.

- I am not Nicola's father but I know that he would have been so proud of her today, as I am.
- Nicola has always been a joy in my life and I am honoured that she chose me to give this speech.
- As Nicola's big brother, I am supposed to be nasty to her and pull her hair to remind her that I am older than she is. Trouble is, she looks too gorgeous today. I am very proud to be giving her away on behalf of our family. John, please look after her!

## 4 Welcome the groom

Here are a few ideas with a number of options to cut and paste into your own speech.

- There are not many men good enough for Nicola, but John is. When she turned up with a *scruffy/spotty/runny-nosed/well-groomed/lanky/large/tall/pony-tailed* man, I was *suspicious/delighted/dismayed/curious/welcoming, and/but I never hoped/really hoped* that they would marry. *And/But* they have and I am thrilled for them. John is a *good/delightful/fun/great/lovely* man and they make a wonderful couple.

- John is one of that rare breed of men – he really is as *good/sincere/wonderful/perfect/much of a creep* as he appears and I am absolutely delighted to welcome him into our/my family.

- Nicola always claimed that she would never *get married/find the right man/love anyone/be happy*, but she was wrong. In John she has found the perfect partner and I am delighted he has become a part of *my/our family*.

- What can I say about John? He is a *great/perfect/lovely/wonderful/good* man and no one else would be as perfect for my *daughter/Nicola*. I'm delighted that he's decided to become part of the family.

## 5 General chat

This is your chance to make a few gentle jokes, but nothing crude or offensive. You might even want to quote something or recite a poem.

- Marriage, as I know all too well, is about compromise and to keep things running smoothly it's good to talk. However, as Helen Rowland said, 'Before marriage, a man will lie awake thinking about something you said; after marriage, he'll fall asleep before you finish saying it.'
- The best guarantee for a peaceful marriage is simple – lie. If she asks you if you've done whatever you've forgotten to do, say that you have and then do it. If he catches you doing something you shouldn't, say you did it as a surprise for him. Men are stupid: they'll believe anything, or at least pretend to, for a peaceful life!
- Nicola always said that she'd never find that special someone, but I'm delighted to see that she has. I just want to read something now because it seems so appropriate and expresses exactly what I mean. It's called *Destiny* and is by Sir Edwin Arnold:

Somewhere there waiteth in this world of ours
For one lone soul another lonely soul,
Each choosing each through all the weary hours
And meeting strangely at one sudden goal.
Then blend they, like green leaves with golden flowers,
Into one beautiful and perfect whole;
And life's long night is ended, and the way
Lies open onward to eternal day.

- You may think that this wedding has cost a lot but, as Goethe said, 'The sum which two married people owe to one another defies calculation. It is an infinite debt which can only be discharged through all eternity.' I wonder if their bank manager would believe that?
- As a certain German philosopher once said: 'To marry is to halve your rights and double your duties', but if that were all there is to it, then none of us would get married in the first place. I'm delighted that Nicola and John have taken the plunge, otherwise none of us would be here enjoying this fine *champagne/wine/ beer/tap water*.

## 6  The toast

By the time you get to the toast, it's almost time for you to sit down – but not quite. Finish with a flourish and then relax – the rest of the day/evening/night is yours to enjoy!

- Ladies and gentlemen, please be upstanding. I give you... the bride and groom.
- Ladies and gentlemen, please charge your glasses. I give you... the bride and groom.
- Honoured guests, please join me in the traditional toast. I give you... the bride and groom.
- Ladies and gentlemen, please be upstanding and raise your glasses. I give you... the bride and groom.

## Sample speech snippets

### He even buys a round

'I haven't known Gary (*the groom*) very long, but I have already been very impressed with him and, in particular, his ability to get a round in at the Horse and Groom.

'Tanya (*the bride*) had told us so much about him before we met him that we were expecting a combination of Brad Pitt, Bill Gates and Stephen Hawking. I should make clear: the looks of Brad Pitt, the financial muscle of Bill Gates, and the intellect of Stephen Hawking.

(*Pause*) 'I'll let you be the judges of that.

'The other thing I remember about meeting Gary for the first time was how terrified Tanya was. In fact she was so nervous that she actually helped with the washing up...'

## How things have changed

'The rules of love and marriage have changed so much since Doris (*the bride's mother*) and I got married.

'We never lived together beforehand, whereas Zoe (*the bride*) and Jack (*the groom*) have been happily cohabiting for the best part of five years.

'Zoe told me the other day that Jack's most endearing habit was to clear her hair out of the plug after she has had a bath. This was not something I could have said to my dad!

'Another difference is that modern couples never talk about money. Have you noticed that? Doris and I used to talk about it all the time, or the lack of it. Did we have enough? Could we afford to go to Benidorm for our holidays or did we have to make do with Paignton?

'Zoe and Jack, on the other hand, don't talk about money – they just spend it. Not that I resent it. After all, I can't take it with me. As Jack is always pointing out...'

## Daddy's girl

'As any dad will tell you, I think there is something special in the bond between a father and his daughter.

'The father cannot believe that any man could possibly be good enough for his daughter. And the daughter has to find a husband who can combine the father's qualities of kindness, love and generosity – and I would emphasize the generosity – which is clearly no mean feat.

'In Billie's (*the bride*) case, though, I think I may have met my match. First of all, Zac (*the groom*) seems to earn more in a day than I earn in a year.

'But much more importantly, he loves her to bits just as much as I do. I've watched him with her – he's like a combination of faithful dog and butler to her... just what I like to see in a son-in-law.'

## He's got his work cut out

'Mike (*the groom*) may think he knows Lucy (*the bride*) very well because they've been going out for three years. But I *lived* with Lucy for 20. I know. And Mike: I have got plenty of advice for you!

'First thing is: don't imagine that you will ever get to the bathroom before Lucy in the morning. I never managed it in two decades. Even as a toddler, she knew how to get in the bathroom first and lock the door.

'Second: don't worry if Lucy goes to sleep at odd times. This is perfectly normal and is not narcolepsy. She once went to sleep *while I was telling her off*. Not that you'll be doing any of that, I'm sure.'

## Second time around

'It gives me great pleasure to be standing in front of you today to propose the health of the bride and groom. As you will know, I've done it before, as this is Charmaine's (*the bride*) second run round the Marriage Course.

'I've told her it's a bit like the Grand National. The first time you do it, you learn how high the fences are and sometimes you fall off. It's nobody's fault. The second time you do it, you know more about how it's done, how to avoid the stray horses and how to get to the finishing line. And, of course, you enjoy it more.'

## Crossing the language barrier

'I know that it's traditional for the father to lament the loss of his daughter. But in this case I know that Samantha (*the bride*) is going to be very happy with Sylvan (*the groom*).

'Sylvan is a very kind boy – he offered to buy me a Zimmer frame the other day – and I know that he will always put his new wife – my daughter – first.

'Sylvan is French, of course, and I have tried very hard to train him in the British way of doing things.

'I've started to teach him the rules of cricket, for example, with the tender hope that in a few years' time we shall be able to sit in the Six Bells at Warnborough and discuss googlies and LBWs.

'Sylvan very gamely played a match for our cricket club the other day, subbing at the last minute for our star bowler who had turned his ankle.

'During our innings, the captain came up to him and said: "Sylvan, you're in." Sylvan replied: "In what?" Captain: "You're in. You're batting." Sylvan: "So what do I have to do?" "Well," said the captain, "you have to go out and bat."

'Sylvan looked at me and said: "I'm in, so I have to go out. It is an impossible language".'

## Of love and marriage

'I was told that one of my tasks in this speech is to give sound advice to the bride and groom about love and marriage. I suppose it depends on whether you believe these things change from one generation to the next.

'Sex has definitely changed. Before I got married, sex was something the upper class got their coal in. (Remember coal, anyone?)

'Love is probably much the same as it ever was, however. In which case my advice is: once you've found it, keep it. Marriage: well, it's only happened to me once and it's the best thing that has ever happened to me.

'My only advice is to remember: the most important thing is give and take. Your wife gives instructions and you take them.'

## Learning to let go

'It was a great shock to me when Kay (*the bride*) announced to my wife Frances (*the bride's mother*) that she was going to get married.

'Not because she was so young – after all, Frances and I were married at about the same age – but because I have always thought of Kay as our little girl, falling over and crying, or climbing apple trees, or mucking about in rock pools at the seaside.

'I was suddenly surprised at the idea that she had outgrown all of those things. So I must admit I shed a little tear at the thought that our Kay was going to flee the nest and set up on her own.

'And, what's more, with another man!

'Of course, Frances was much more laid-back about it all. "That'll save money on the bills," was her first reaction.

'But I'm going to miss Kay: I'm going to miss her leaving the fridge door open all night after a midnight plunder of our food supplies; I'm going to miss those late-night phone calls asking me to come and pick her up from the station because she's missed the last bus and hasn't got the money for a taxi; and I'm going to miss the incessant racket coming from her bedroom...

'On second thoughts, I think I'll be all right.'

## Money matters

'I was chatting to Patrick (*the groom*) the other day. He still has some touchingly naïve ideas about Jane (*the bride*).

'For example, he hasn't fitted a padlock yet to his wallet. He was talking about opening a joint bank account, but I soon put a stop to that.

'I told him to make sure he had plenty of cash on him whenever he and Jane go out together. Don't go to markets that sell clothes. Don't go to markets full stop. Don't go anywhere that might possibly, conceivably, try to sell you anything, like a shop.

'Delegate that to somebody like the Queen, who never carries any money with her.'

## Meet the parents

'The first time that Boris (*the groom*) came to lunch was a slightly fraught moment for everybody.

'Of course, we all know now that Boris is the most wonderful, kind-hearted chap you could imagine, but on that occasion he was rather nervous and an unknown quantity.

'The first thing that happened was that he knocked a vase off the hall table... not a very valuable one, you understand, only a couple of grand.

'Then he accidentally trod on our dog Cherry, who, I must admit, does have a habit of getting under people's feet. Luckily, Boris offered to go 50:50 on the vet's fees.

'And then finally, when his offer to do the washing-up had been politely but firmly refused (avoid collateral damage is my motto), he managed to knock down the gazebo in the back garden.

'I still don't know to this day how he managed to do it. It was like we were getting Frank Spencer as our future son-in-law.

'But the funny thing was that all this only made me like him more. And the thing that really convinced me was Helen's (*the bride*) face as he tried to apologize. The more he devastated her parents' house, the more her eyes shone.'

# Toasts given by the father of the bride

The father of the bride traditionally toasts the bride and groom at the end of his speech.

## A traditional approach

'Today is all about two people and their decision to spend the rest of their lives together. We wish them good luck and great joy, today and always. So please stand and raise your glasses with me... To the happy couple!'

'I end my speech today by thanking you all for joining us to celebrate the wedding of Annabel and Ben. It's been a wonderful day so far and we hope this will be the beginning of a wonderful life together for them. Please join me in wishing them all the best... To Annabel and Ben!'

## Bit of banter

'Before we raise our glasses, John, I'd like you to take Diana's hand and place your own over it. Now remember and cherish this special moment, because believe me, if I know my daughter, this is the last time you'll have the upper hand... To Diana and John!'

## Quick quip

'Apparently, my wife tells me, I'm now supposed to make toast. Good grief! Haven't you all eaten enough already?'

'Ah, right, I see, I'm supposed to make a toast. Well, then, please stand and raise your glasses quickly before I mess anything else up and join with me In wishing John and Emma every happiness... To the bride and groom!'

## Getting sentimental

'It's said that when children find true love, parents find true joy – and true joy is what I am feeling today. As a father, whatever else I may have wanted for my children, my abiding wish has always been for them to find relationships in which they can be truly happy. I know Katie has found this with Daniel. Katie, as everyone knows, is the apple of my eye. So for me to say that I have gained a wonderful son-in-law is the greatest compliment that I can give. Ladies and gentlemen, I would like you to join me in drinking a toast to the happy couple. Please be upstanding and raise your glasses to Katie and Daniel.'

# The groom's speech

# The groom

You will say the most important words of the day, if not your life, when you say 'I do'.

Now it's your chance to thank everybody and tell your bride how much you love her, and in front of all your family and friends.

Daunted? Don't be – everybody is there because they want to be. They've chosen to spend their free time watching you marry the woman you love and, for once, the focus is not on her dress but on you.

Remember that if your bride is not going to give a speech, all your words should be from both of you. Make this clear throughout your speech – you don't want to just include your new wife in a single section of it as if you'd only just remembered her at the last minute! Oh – and beginning your speech with, 'My wife and I...' usually provokes an immediate audience reaction!

## When to speak

Traditionally, you speak second – after the father of the bride and before the best man and any other speakers.

### What to say
- Thank the father of the bride for his (hopefully) kind comments!
- Thank the wedding organizers/mums – often with bouquets.
- Thank everyone for being there.
- Compliment your new wife.
- Toast the bridesmaids, often giving them a gift.

### Alternatives
But you don't have to stick with tradition. You could:
- Let the bride speak instead, or do the speech together.
- Read out a poem that sums up how you feel about the day.
- Simply toast those who helped with the wedding, but don't make a speech.

# The basics

The groom's speech is the place to thank everyone who has helped to make the day special and to thank the guests for gifts on behalf of yourself and your new wife.

Your speech is also where the groom gets to say something lovely about the bride. Often too, you'll make a last-minute comedy plea for mercy from the best man.

If you feel up to it, you can also introduce some funny stories – but make them touching rather than too risqué. Don't use these stories as an excuse not to say what you feel about your wife.

You'll probably want to say something about how you met, about how your relationship developed, perhaps something about love and marriage.

Many grooms find it difficult to speak about their feelings so publicly, but a few brief words, spoken from the heart, is all it takes. Quoting a poem or a song lyric to help you express how you feel is perfectly acceptable.

## What is expected of the groom?

In your speech, you will usually:

- Thank your father-in-law for his speech and for his beautiful daughter.
- Thank both sets of parents for all their help in the wedding preparations.
- Give a small gift to the two mothers. (For some suggestions, see www.confetti.co.uk)
- Thank the guests for sharing your day and for their generous gifts.
- Thank other people who have helped with the wedding.
- Compliment your new wife and express your feelings for her.
- Thank the best man for his help/support/drinks and beg him to be nice to you.
- Raise a glass and offer a toast to the bridesmaids.

## Useful phrases

Here are some useful phrases and ideas for a great groom's speech. All you need to do is pick the best ones for you and fill in the blanks!

## Thank your new father-in-law

- I just want to thank my father-in-law for his *kind/generous/special* words. I feel honoured that he has *taken/welcomed* me into his family.
- Thank you, Ken, for your *kind/generous/sweet/special* words. It is good to know how you feel about Sarah and me getting married.
- My wife and I would like to thank Ken for being the best father of the bride ever. Not only did he give her away instead of locking her in her room, but his *kind/sweet/generous/witty* words have also made me feel welcome as the newest member of his family.
- My wife and I want to thank Ken for his *witty/kind/ generous/sincere* words. I now feel *embarrassed about everything I said about him in the past/justified in my opinion that he's a great/good/perfect* father-in-law. What can I say after that speech? Thanks, Ken.

## 2 Thank your guests

- This is the most important day of our lives, and my wife and I/*Sarah and I/we* are delighted to share it with *so many friends and family/our closest friends and families/two complete strangers in a register office.* We are also very grateful that so many of you have not only gone to the expense of sharing this day with us but have also bought us presents. Thank you.
- I can't believe that you all made it here. You really are the best *bunch/group/lot/mob/pack/herd* of friends and family that we could ever hope to have. So thank you. We're also extremely grateful for the presents. Sarah was saying only a couple of days ago that she really wanted another toaster... or two!

## 3 Thank your in-laws

- I am so *delighted/pleased/honoured/relieved/happy* to have Ken and Angela as my *new family/in-laws/other Mum and Dad.* I knew that I'd *like/love/get on with/adore* them when I fell in love with Sarah because they have helped her to be the person she is – *perfect/rich/wonderful/fond of beer and rugby!*

## 4 Compliment your wife!

- You are always beautiful but you have never looked as *stunning/good/wonderful/gorgeous* as you do today. You make the most *wonderful/stunning/gorgeous/perfect* bride. I love you.
- I was expecting to feel *nervous/sick/terrified/concerned/worried/frightened* when I woke up today but I didn't. Why? Because I knew that you would be walking down that aisle towards me and that the only thing I wanted was for *you to be my wife/us to be married.* I knew that you would look lovely – you always do – but today you are *radiant/*

gorgeous/beautiful/wonderful/fantastic/stunning/a vision/ perfect/the perfect bride. You mean so much to me, and I want to thank you for agreeing to become my wife. I am so proud/happy/honoured to be your husband, and I love you very much.

- Sarah, you are a beautiful/stunning/radiant/gorgeous/lovely bride, and I know that you are just as beautiful on the inside. When we first met, I realized that you were the most beautiful woman in the world/were the only woman for me/had a ladder in your stockings, but I never thought/imagined/dared to hope that you would marry me. I am so happy/chuffed/ delighted/ecstatic/proud that you agreed to be my wife and share the rest of your life with me. I've been so proud of the way you have juggled organizing this wedding with your job/everything else and have still been patient and understanding. Now, I just want to say, in front of our friends and family, how much you mean to me. I love you.

- The first time I saw Hannah I was dazzled by her. If you had told me then that we would one day be married, I wouldn't have believed you – although I would have wanted to. I can honestly say that I don't think anyone could be as happy as I am today. I'm immensely proud to be able to call her my wife. What I really love about our relationship is that we make a really great team. We trust and support one another, and we each know that, come what may, the other will be there for them. I know that marriage is not all about fun and laughter like today, but I know too that my wife and I have the strength to deal with any difficulties that life may throw at us.

## 5 Thank your bride

- I never thought I could be as happy as I am today without *England/Wales/Scotland/Ireland* winning the Six Nations. Roz, you've made me feel like I've *scored the winning try/kicked a critical drop goal* in the match of my life. You're my *Twickenham/Millennium Stadium/Murrayfield/Lansdowne Road*, and right now I feel like cheering because I'm just over the moon you've married me. I know there will be times when you send me *for an early bath/to sit in the sin bin*. But I also know that, just like supporting Bath, it's something that stays with you for life, through the ups and downs, and you just can't change that. Roz, I'm your biggest fan, and I love you. (You can amend the above to reflect your favourite sport – but only use it if it's not a sore spot with the bride!)

## 6 Thank the best man

- When I asked Sarah to marry me, I knew that I needed a best man and that there was only one man that title could be given to. Bob *is my brother and also a friend/has been my best friend since school/1972/we met in the sandpit/he stole my BMX*, and I knew that he would be perfect for the job. I would like to thank him for all the work he's done today – *acting as toastmaster/not losing the rings/getting me to the church on time/finding my trousers* – and for his efforts before the wedding when he listened to me as I raved about the latest *waistcoat/buttonhole/wedding suit* I had seen. Bob, you've been *great/a mate/the best man I could have chosen/cool/a pal/a true friend/gorgeous!*

• I get the fun parts of today, but Bob has all the stressful parts. As he's the *local postie/hippo-keeper/accountant/general layabout*, I knew that he would be more than able to cope with today and keep everything, especially me, ticking along smoothly.

## 7  Thank and toast the bridesmaids

• The *giggling little posse/stunning group of beautiful bridesmaids over there/to my right/to my left/in front of you* have been amazing. Not only did they manage to walk down the aisle without falling over, but they've also been great with all the preparations. It may seem unfair to the rest of you, as you've all been *so great/helpful/amazing/bored rigid*, but I'd particularly like to thank Vikki for all her hard work. I understand that Sarah's dress would not be looking quite *so beautiful/stunning/together/white* as it does now were it not for a timely intervention! Ladies and gentleman, I'd like you all *to charge/raise your glasses*. I give you... the bridesmaids.

• *My wife and I/Sarah* and I would like to say a special thank you to the bridesmaids, who have been a tower of strength throughout the *preparations/day*. They've been *great/wonderful/beautiful*, and little Anna has been so *good/patient/sweet and looks gorgeous/adorable/very grown up* in her dress. Ladies and gentlemen, please charge/raise your glasses. I give you... the bridesmaids.

## Sample speech snippets

### Love at first sight

'I am not afraid to admit that I adored Francesca (*the bride*) from the very moment I saw her. The fact that this happened on Archway tube station did not change things one bit. I thought to myself: 'That's a person I could spend the rest of my life with.'

'And since that moment, that feeling hasn't changed an iota. (I looked up "iota" on Google, by the way, and it refers to the Indiana Occupational Therapy Association.)

'They say that love at first sight is an illusion, but I know that it isn't. They say that when you meet the person you're destined to love, you have the feeling that you know them already. That's what happened to me.'

### I'd like to thank my in-laws...

'Among the many people I have to thank today, the most important are Jack and Linda (*the bride's parents*). For without them, of course, there would be no Sally (*the bride*), no wedding, and so... no groom's speech, which would doubtless be a tragic loss to you all.

'Jack and Linda have been tremendously kind and supportive to us in our relationship and especially in the preparations for today. They really have been an absolute tower of strength, and I would like, on behalf of Sally and me, to say a big thank you to them. We don't know how we'd have managed everything without them.'

## He really is the best man

'I'd like to thank Quentin (*the best man*) for all his work behind the scenes today.

'He is really a supportive and loyal friend. He wasn't late for the church, he didn't lose the rings, and he didn't write his speech at the last minute, unlike some people!

'Rumour has it that he is planning to tell some very rude (and completely untrue) stories about me in his speech; that he is planning to get the DJ to play "The birdie song" as our first dance; and that he is planning to put a piece of fish in the hottest part of the engine of our car just before we drive off for the honeymoon.

'But I know he isn't going to do any of those things. Because Quentin is a loyal and supportive friend, AREN'T YOU, MR FLOPPY-DRAWERS?'

## Not as bad as all that

'Those of you who are married will know that, although you are obviously looking forward to the day very much, there is always a certain nervousness beforehand.

'I read somewhere that one in 65 grooms drops the ring down the toilet in the two weeks before the wedding. But the article missed out a few key points.

'It didn't say, for instance, whether it was more common to drop the groom's ring or the bride's ring down the pan.

'And it didn't answer my first question, which was: what were they doing with the ring in the toilet? Taking it out to admire it? Checking it was still there... oops, it's not there any more?

'And the 64-million-dollar question – did they flush it away and go out and buy a new one, or did they fish it out, clean it up and pretend nothing had happened?

'How many brides today are wandering around with rings which... no, no, no, this way madness lies.

'I just want Delia (*bride*) to realize that things could have been much worse than a little thing like the groom forgetting to book the honeymoon...'

## Reasons to be cheerful

'It's wonderful to be here and share this lovely day with you all. Now I was looking through a book of quotations to find some inspiration for my speech, and I came across this from a lady called Rita Rudner. "Men with a pierced ear are better prepared for marriage. They've experienced pain and bought jewellery."

'Well, I think that's a little pessimistic. I see a wedding as a moment of hope. It's when you put your trust in the future, you throw off the dull constraints of everyday life and say to the whole world: we can make our lives better!'

## For a second marriage (following divorce)

'I keep thinking of that clever if a touch cynical sentiments of Samuel Johnson's: "A second marriage is the triumph of hope over experience". Well, I would say that this second marriage is "the triumph of experience over hope".

'If that sounds a bit odd, let me explain what I mean. Of course, if your first marriage did not work out well, you are rather wary of putting yourself through the same thing again. But it won't be the same thing, because the experience of the first marriage will help you to win through in the second.'

## For a second marriage (following death of partner)

'As many of you will know, my first wife Ada died about seven years ago, at the age of 44.

'At the time, I was so devastated, I not only thought that I would never marry again, I almost vowed that I wouldn't. It seemed like disrespect to Ada and her memory.

'However, with the passing of time, I've come to realize two things – one is that, as they say, time heals all wounds. The other is that love is not divisible. It's not something that if you give some of it to one person, then another person has to have less.

'I don't love Ada any less because I now love Olivia (*the bride*). And of course Ada is the first person who would have told me this.'

## So what if it all goes wrong?

'I want to thank especially Ken and Marty (*the bride's parents*). Apart from anything else, they paid for the whole show! But not only that – they have helped in all kinds of small ways as well... a hundred-and-one little things that all add up to the strongest show of support any groom could ever possibly hope to receive.

'Marty even sewed a button back on my morning suit while we were waiting in the church. (Actually in the time it took the bridal car to arrive, she could have rustled up a whole set of bridesmaids' dresses...)

'Ken and Marty have the inestimable quality of total unflappability. For instance, I said to Ken on Wednesday evening: "What if something goes wrong on Saturday?" To which he replied: "That'll make everything go better. People enjoy a disaster".'

## With a friend like this...

'Well, everything seems to be going very well today, and both Mary (*the bride*) and I hope you will all have a lovely day. I should thank Hal (*the best man*) for his sterling efforts of organization, but actually, well, Hal seems to have his own agenda this week.

'On Monday he rang me to say he wouldn't be able to be the best man after all, as he was leaving for Tanzania. This seemed a very elaborate and expensive way to get out of being best man. On Tuesday he rang to say he'd got the dates wrong and Tanzania was next week.

'On Wednesday he was late for the stag night and missed the first round. On Thursday he rang up to say that the reason he had been late for the stag night was because he had been looking for the ring and he still hadn't found it.

'Yesterday evening, he rang to say that he had found it, in that special hiding place which he uses to keep special items of value and which he can never remember where it is. (His wallet.)

'And finally, at 9am this morning he rang me to ask whether the church was St James's or St John's. I told him it was St Andrew's.'

## Where we met

'I have been asked many times where I met Diana (*the bride*) and it's a strange fact that I have never told anybody. And today I can reveal exclusively... that we actually met in a brothel.

'Now before you get any funny ideas – we didn't know it was a brothel at the time. And neither of us was there... you know. The fact is that I was working for a building company and I got a call from the local council to say there was a potentially unsafe building in – well, perhaps I'd better not say where it was in case any of you live there – part of Nottingham, and could I go there with the council officer to check it out?

'Diana was that council officer. We checked the building, found it was fine, went for a coffee together, and the rest is history. It was only later, much later, when the building was pulled down to build a block of flats, that it came out that it was a place where the ladies of the night plied their trade. So I suppose you could say that every cloud has a silver lining.'

# Toasts given by the groom

The groom traditionally toasts the bridesmaids/maid of honour. He may also choose to toast his wife; his wife will then reply and toast the bridesmaids. He may also toast the hosts, traditionally his new in-laws, especially if there are no bridesmaids.

### Edible joke

'Apparently I'm now supposed to toast our hosts, my parents-in-law. That's a bit of a shame because I think I'd rather have them spit-roasted with onions and lots of garlic. Oh, that kind of toast. Awfully sorry, Mr and Mrs Johnson: you know I think you're good enough to eat! To Mr and Mrs Johnson, ladies and gentlemen!'

## Thanks, ladies

'I'd like to take this opportunity to thank the bridesmaids for their sterling work. I've discovered that for an occasion like this, you really do need to have experts on table flowers, leg-waxing, eyelash-curling and themed party favours on hand, and Alice, Hannah and Ellen certainly fit the bill. They really have been essential in making this a perfect day. Ladies and gentlemen, please raise your glasses to the bridesmaids.'

## One for the parents

'A wedding is a coming together of two families, and I couldn't have wished to join a friendlier family than Stella's, so I'd like to end my speech by thanking our hosts and my new parents-in-law, Betty and Stan, for making this such a wonderful occasion. It's often said that wedding days belong to the happy couple, but there are many people who have helped to make today so perfect. I'd also like to thank my parents, Pauline and Max, for everything they've done for us. Without the hard work of our parents, Stella and I wouldn't have been able to concentrate on having such a good time today! Please raise your glasses to them.'

## Love lines

'I'd like to end my speech by proposing a toast to my bride. Without wishing to embarrass anyone by getting too sentimental, Charlotte is all I have ever dreamed of. Someone once said that to love is to receive a glimpse of heaven. Well, I feel I am truly in heaven today... Please raise your glasses to the beautiful bride.'

# The
# best
# man's
## speech

# The best man

The best man's speech is often the most eagerly anticipated and attentively listened to of all. So it's not surprising that making the speech has become the centrepiece of the best man's role and is likely to dominate the way in which you prepare for the big day.

Your role is a multiple one. As the groom's best friend, you will be expected to subject him to an ordeal of gentle embarrassment. And as traditional head of the wedding assistants, you will also speak on behalf of the bridesmaids, read out telegrams and pass on any practical announcements, as well as introducing all the other speakers, unless there is a toastmaster.

Nowadays, it's becoming more usual for other people to make a speech – the mother of the bride and chief bridesmaid, for example, might want to say a few words.

## When to speak

Traditionally, you are the final speaker of the day. However many people speak, the best man always goes last – saving the best till then, hopefully.

## What to say

You'll want to make your speech as entertaining as possible, but traditionally the best man's speech is also expected to cover certain points.

- Read out any messages from friends and family who haven't been able to attend.
- Propose a toast to the bride and groom.
- Thank the groom for his toast to the bridesmaids.
- Talk about the happy couple, particularly the groom.
- Comment on how great the day has been.
- Thank the organizers.

## Alternatives

- Traditionally the best man makes the speech solo, but nowadays it's not unusual to make a joint speech with the ushers, other friends or the chief bridesmaid.
- You can consider performing a stunt with the aid of a few props, using a home video or slides, or invent some funny telegrams.

# The basics

Speeches are usually made after the main meal, so by the time the best man comes to speak, the guests tend to have relaxed considerably (a fact not unconnected with the amount of wine that has been consumed!). This can often work in your favour, as by now the guests will be nicely warmed up and well disposed to laugh at your jokes. Remember, they're not expecting a professional stand-up – they want to enjoy themselves and will be with you every step of the way.

The best man's speech shouldn't be too long. A few short stories told clearly and warmly, will go down much better than a rambling speech.

A word about content... it's tempting as best man to feel that your job is to torture the groom by uncovering everything you know about him that he'd rather no one knew. But resist the temptation to take it too far.

Above all, remember the golden rule: don't be anything but positive about the bride. Increasingly best men are making their speeches as much about the bride as the groom, with stories of how the best man and the bride first met, the (very positive) effect the bride has had on the groom, how pleased they are to see their mate so lucky in love, and so on.

## Useful phrases

Here are some useful phrases and ideas for a best man's speech. All you need to do is pick the best ones for you and fill in the blanks!

## 1 The thanks

You represent the other members of the bridal party (the bridesmaids and ushers), so the first thing you have to say is easy – thank the groom for his words about the bridesmaids.

- Ladies and gentlemen, I would like to thank the groom for his *kind/generous/short/patronizing/lying* words about the *lovely/giggling/drunken/fabulous* bridesmaids.

## 2 Who are you?

Let everyone know how you and the groom first met each other and how you feel about being his best man.

- When I first met John on our first day at *school/uni/prison /work*, I thought that he was *a good bloke/a con man/an idiot/an alcoholic/a lucky man to meet me*, but I never realized that I would end up, all these years later, being his best man. I have to say that I was *honoured/staggered/horrified/shocked/ drunk* when he asked me, but I'm *delighted/honoured/pleased/ drunk again/terrified* to be here today in front of all of you.

## 3 About the groom

- John has always been *a good bloke/an idiot/a generous man*, even when *(say when you met, for example, first day of school)* and he (recount a funny incident or use one of his pet phrases; don't cause offence but be funny). I can't believe that he's *finally/actually* married.
- When John asked me to be his best man I thought that *he had no other friends/his Mum had made him ask me*, and I was *honoured/terrified*. Now that I'm here, I'm even more so.
- The man who wouldn't *commit/buy pizza for more than one/ share his remote control/even consider a joint bank account* is now married!

• I never thought that I'd live to see this day. I've known John since (say how you met and when) and I'm *delighted/ stunned/pleased/shocked/really happy* for him and even more *shocked at/horrified at/staggered by/terrified by/ committed* to being his best man – as he is the best man I've ever known.

## 4 Tell an amusing/sweet anecdote about the groom

You're his best man for a reason, so delve into your mutual past and tell an amusing anecdote. Hopefully, the only difficulty doing this will be trying to decide which one to tell. If it's not that easy, the following might trigger a few memories – just remember to keep it short and clean!

• When he had to think up an original excuse for being late/not handing in his homework/project.

• The first time you had a boy's night out and he decided that he wanted to be a morris dancer.

• His dreams of unsuitable jobs, for example, pilot, stripper (unless he was!), train/racing driver (and recently had a minor scrape in his car), pop star (and can't sing), etc.

• Cooking anecdotes always work. The late Dame Barbara Cartland once said that 90 per cent of marriages end because of bad cooking: even if he didn't blow up a microwave by putting a whole egg in it, he must have had some kind of cooking disaster – we all have. As the 19th-century novelist George Meredith said, 'Kissing don't last: cookery do!'

### 5  Don't forget the bride

Always make a point of saying something nice about the bride. This is the woman who will let your friend/brother still go out to play with the lads, so start off on the right foot. You know you want to!

- *Sarah/Mrs Finn* is the luckiest *woman/girl* for marrying John today, but, looking at her, I can understand why he chose her. She's a *beautiful/stunning/gorgeous/lovely/radiant bride.*
- Sarah, what can I say? You look *beautiful/lovely/stunning/ radiant* and you *deserve each other/make a beautiful couple/are perfect for each other.*
- When John first introduced me to Sarah, my first reaction was that she was *too good/perfect/ideal* for him. I'm delighted to see them here together today and wish them every happiness for the future.

## 6  Telegram time

A simple rule: explain who all the telegrams are from. Bill and Joy Patterson may mean nothing to many people, and saying Uncle Bill and Aunt Joy from Scotland will make it easier for everyone.

### 7  Almost there – the final toast

It's nearly time to sit down, but not just yet. This is the easy bit and your audience will be delighted to participate. Decide with the bride and groom beforehand if people should stand up or not. If they should, ask them to 'be upstanding'.

- Ladies and gentlemen, please be upstanding and *raise/charge* your glasses. I give you... the bride and groom.
- Ladies and gentlemen, please join me in a toast. I give you... the bride and groom.

# Do's and don'ts

- Never swear or use offensive words, even if they do crop up in everyday speech.
- Always think of an old granny sitting in the corner when you write your speech and try not to give her a heart attack or make her blush!
- Don't try too hard to be funny.
- Avoid saying anything you wouldn't want anyone to know if it were about you, and you can't go wrong.
- Make a note of anyone you want to thank or mention. You might find it easiest to write down your speech, for either glancing at or as reassurance, or use little revision cards with bullet point reminders.
- Decide if you want to read some cards or telegrams during your speech. If you do, be sure to arrange for a family member to collect them together for you.
- Practise, practise, practise!
- Never make fun of the wedding – even if you dislike the venue, colour scheme, bridesmaid's dresses.
- Avoid potentially difficult and embarrassing subjects such as having children (in case it turns out that they can't), drug problems (in case either the bride or the families don't know about it), excessive partying or womanizing while seeing the bride (ditto), money problems (ditto) or previous girlfriends (need we say more?).

# Sample speech snippets

## My brother, the groom

'It's rather disconcerting to stand here and talk about Lawrence (*the groom*) entering the state of holy matrimony.

'As his brother, I look back on our childhood together – he's only two years older than me – and think of when Lawrence would beat up his friend who lived next door (little Mary, aged 4). Was this a man who loves and esteems women?

'I think of when we were both grounded for a week by Dad – if memory serves, for putting lighted fireworks in Mr Brown-at-no.16's slippers during bob-a-job week – and Lawrence escaped out of the house and over the garden fence to go to the pub, and think: is this a man who will want to be shackled by the bonds of marriage?

'And so with a brother's long memory and fond affection I look across at Rose, his charming new bride, and I say to myself: "*What was she thinking?*"'

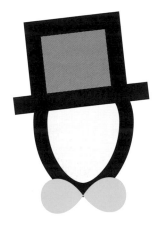

## Portrait of the groom as a young man

'Obviously, being Neil's (*the groom*) brother, I've got a lot of stories from his youth that will give Teresa (*the bride*) a better idea of what she is letting herself in for.

'But it's not all bad, Teresa!

'He's very loyal: witness the time he absolutely refused to tell the police which of his friends had been with him on the shoplifting trip to Asda in High Wycombe.

'He's determined: he once queued for 52 minutes to get a pint of bitter at the Test Match. (I know, because it was my pint.)

'And he's resourceful: when we were six, he managed to get over the 8-foot wall at the end of our garden, unaided, even by a ladder, in order to rescue our football which had gone over the wall.

'It was just a shame there was a greenhouse at the very point he jumped down from.'

## Generous to a fault

'Angela (*the bride*) is one of the loveliest, sweetest-natured people I know and I'm sure that she and Howard (*the groom*) are going to be very happy together. Howard, if you ever have second thoughts, I'll be pleased to take her off your hands.

'Just one story I can tell to illustrate Angela's kindness: the three of us were walking through Bonn Square one day when a homeless man said to us "Have you got 50p?" Howard and I replied "Yes, thanks," and walked on, but Angela went to the nearest sandwich bar, bought a sandwich and a drink, and gave them to the man.

'Afterwards I rather facetiously asked her if she did that with everyone who asked her for money, and she replied: "Why, are you peckish?" That told me.'

## Footballer's wife

I first met Gloria (*the bride*) at Queen's Park Rangers football ground. She's a supporter, which immediately told me that, as a wife, she would be steadfast in times of difficulty, would fight against any odds for her loved ones, and was probably also stark raving bonkers.

That last quality's probably quite important, now that's she married to Jon (*the groom*).

And even though QPR play in what is effectively the Second Division (*update as appropriate*) I'm sure their marriage will be Premiership in every way!

## On the horns of a dilemma

'I'm actually on the horns of a dilemma here, because I've been offered large amounts of money by Chris (*the groom*) not to reveal what happened on the stag night on Tuesday. But at the same time, I've been offered even larger amounts by the other participants to tell you all about it...

'Actually, nothing really dramatic happened. I don't call a broken window and a sprained ankle dramatic. A top-speed police chase with blue lights flashing, now THAT would be dramatic, but as far as I remember... anyway the police were very nice about it, considering the number of times they were called out.

'Chris said to me on Wednesday that police cells are actually much more comfortable than most people say. He couldn't get much of a signal on his mobile "inside", but I think that was more because he had dropped it in the goldfish pond in the pub garden.

'To drop your mobile in a goldfish pond is unfortunate, as Oscar Wilde might have said. But to drop yourself in there, in a freak accident involving a go-kart and an inflatable banana... well, that's just careless.'

## Eyewitness account

'We had a marvellous stag night last night. It's not often that I enjoy being the driver on these occasions, but being completely 100 per cent sober gave me the chance to observe Matt (*the groom*) and his friends at close quarters, and also to be able to actually recall some of the stories to tell you about them today.

'And the funny thing is... even though they knew that I was going to tell all 350 assembled wedding guests exactly what they got up to, they still went ahead and got up to it! (*Lead into stories...*)'

## Holiday romance

'They say that when you make friends with somebody on holiday, it is not a relationship that is likely to last, let alone lead to marriage and eternal bliss. Well, marriage anyway.

'And, to be frank, a camping holiday in Scandinavia is not the kind of scenario where you expect to meet the man or woman of your dreams.

'But that's where Sheila and Dougie (*the bride and groom*) met. However – and I don't think I'm giving away any secrets here – the amazing part of the story is that Sheila had taken a little black dress with her to Norway. I mean, what kind of foresight do you need for *that*?'

## A meeting of hearts, minds and souls

'As many of you will know, Peter and Amanda (*the bride and groom*) met when they were both doing charity work in Africa.

'I know from what they have said subsequently that, even though they are both very experienced campaigners, going to Africa and seeing the suffering was a traumatic experience for both of them. But they recognized in each other a like-minded soul, and their friendship helped to get them through a difficult time.

'Over time, that friendship has blossomed, and the work they have done together has brought them ever closer, and I know that their colleagues are always amazed at how their shared experiences seem to bring them closer together.'

## A bit of a reputation

'I know that Charlie (*the groom*) has a little bit of a reputation
as a fun-loving, happy-go-lucky sort of chap. Well, let me tell
you now that nothing could be further from the truth.

'When he set fire to my underpants at the stag party
on Wednesday, he was actually protesting against the
exploitation of workers in Third World sweatshops.

'When he covered the faculty WCs with cling-film in his
last year at University, he was merely testing the stretching
powers of PVC in a controlled scientific experiment.

'When he borrowed my car last week to go on a day trip
to Brighton, how was he to know that I might need it myself?

'(By the way, Jane, (*the bride*), you may not have known
about the day trip to Brighton, but I can assure you it wasn't
what you're thinking...)'

## Joint speech with another best man

'We thought it might be fun if we gave you a quick
demonstration of how Keith (*the groom*) has changed over
the years, so I'll illustrate how he used to be – with a few
stories thrown in as evidence – and Rick (*the other best man*)
will show you what he's like *now*.

'We think you'll see that it's a case of "Plus ça change,
plus c'est la même chose", which is a kind of heavy sauce
containing blueberries.

'Best man 1: 'Keith was a very serious young man. He once
went on hunger strike as a protest against hangovers.

'Best man 2: 'Now he's much more easy-going. When
there's a demo in Trafalgar Square, he films it for CNN...'
(*change as appropriate*).

# Classic best man's toasts

'So I'd like you all to charge your glasses and join me in toasting the new Mr and Mrs Brown. Ladies and gentlemen, I give you the bride and groom.'

'Wishing them all the health, wealth and happiness in the world, I'd like you all to join me in toasting the happy couple. Ladies and gentlemen, the bride and groom.'

'Now it only remains for me to get you all on your feet. And with charged glasses [pause], I'd like you to join me in a toast to the new Mr and Mrs Roberts. Ladies and gentlemen, I give you the wonderful bride and groom.'

'And now all I have left to do is to say what a privilege it is to ask you all to charge your glasses and – for those of you who still can! – rise to your feet. Ladies and gentlemen – the bride and groom.'

'Ladies and gentlemen, will you please join me now in toasting two young – well, quite young! – people who have everything, because (*looks at couple*) you love each other. Ladies and gentlemen, the lucky couple.'

'To finish with some words from the bard: "Love comforteth like sunshine after rain." So, you two, I hope your marriage is full of intermittent drizzle, followed by days of blistering heat. To the bride and groom.'

'To the adorable couple – Mark and Lisa.'

'Jerry – my best friend - here are some words of
advice in the form of a wise old poem. "To keep a
marriage brimming with love in the loving cup, when
you are wrong, admit it, and when you are right, shut
up!" To Jerry and Claire!'

'Here's to the two things that – without doubt – make
a great marriage. Here's to a good sense of humour,
and selective hearing. Ladies and gentlemen – the bride
and groom.'

'Before we toast the happy
couple, here's to wives and lovers
everywhere – and to them
never, ever meeting!'

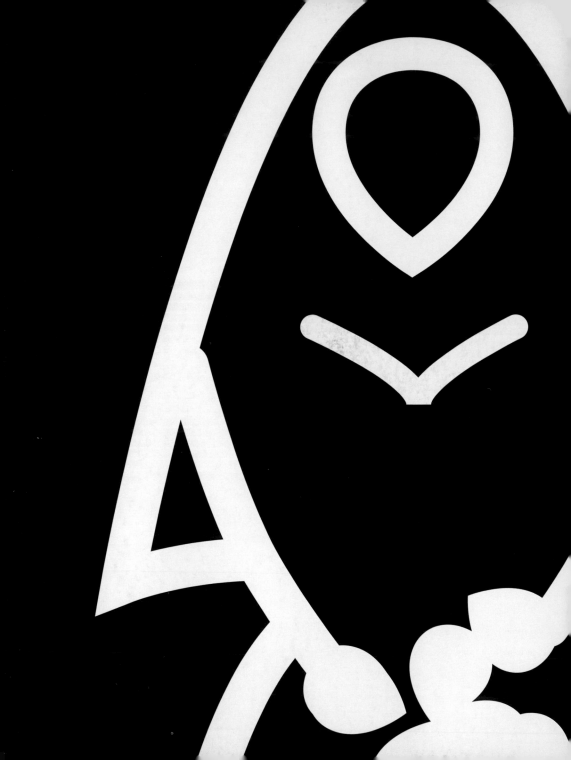

# The
# bride's
## speech

# The bride

More brides are choosing to speak at their wedding these days. As the bride, you have possibly the most interesting role when it comes to making a speech. The other main speeches – the father of the bride, best man and so on – have huge traditions attached to them. But, if you decide to make a speech, there will be no such expectations upon you. Many brides now choose to give a personal speech and it can be a great way of mopping up any forgotten thank yous.

## When to speak

The bride will usually speak just before or after the groom. If you're happy to break with tradition, you may even decide to say a few words at the very end, after the best man, who is usually the last speaker. If your father is not present, then you may want to speak first of all, in the traditional father-of-the-bride slot.

### What to say

- Reiterate thanks already given – especially for gifts.
- Thank anyone who has not already been thanked by other speakers or may not be mentioned by them.
- Mirror the groom's speech – how you met, how the relationship developed.
- Include a personal message to the groom.

### Alternatives

- You may decide to make a joint speech with the groom (in many ways a very logical choice).
- If you and the groom are speaking separately, you could decide in advance to each address different or mirroring themes (the other's family, for instance).

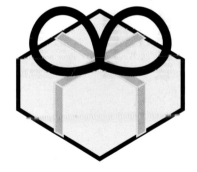

# The basics

As the bride giving a speech is a relatively new tradition, it gives you more scope in what you say. Basically, the bride has an open field. Unlike the best man (who has to humiliate the groom) or the bride's father (who has to get tearful about his daughter), you can say pretty much what you like! Often the bride's speech is memorable for this reason.

Most brides will really want to mention their mum. Thank her for her help in the build-up to the day. You could include something about your relationship over the years. You might also want to thank the bridesmaids (rather than leaving this to the groom – after all, the bridesmaids were helping *you*!) and/or to propose a toast to the guests.

**What to include in your speech**

- Thank everyone who's attending, especially long-lost friends and people who've travelled a long way.
- Thank those people who've supported you through the stress of preparing for the wedding.
- A special word about your mum, not just to thank her for her role in the wedding preparations, but to describe your relationship with her over the years.
- If you like, you could echo the pattern of your new husband's speech: how you met; your first impressions; things you liked and didn't like about him; how the relationship developed; your thoughts on love and marriage; a more personal message from you to him.
- Thank your guests for all their gifts (if the groom hasn't done so already).
- If you are thanking other people, it might make more sense for you, rather than the groom, to thank the bridesmaids.
- A popular American innovation is for the bride to finish with a toast to the guests.

# Sample speech snippets

## Me and my groom

'I want to tell you that Ray (*the groom*) is the most easy-going, lovable cheerful man you could ever hope to meet. He's like a favourite easy chair – comfortable if a bit battered!

'I knew that he was a person that I could spend the rest of my life with when I met his mum and dad, Hillary and Joe. They made me feel at home from the moment I walked through the door. Hillary made me six cups of tea in two hours. And I bet you can guess how many of those cups Ray washed up!'

## Dirty laundry

'As you know, Derek (*the groom*) and I have been living together for two years, so I've got to know some of his more... interesting habits.

'Of course, I promised him faithfully that I wouldn't reveal the more disgusting ones, so see me afterwards if you want the gen. But let me just say that if you need your bath clogging up with toenails, or your bedroom floor strewn with dirty clothes, well, Derek is your man.

'Actually, of course, Derek is *my* man, so hands off!'

## Thanks for everything, mum

'You all know that without my mum, none of the three of us would have got through the last few years.

'Since my father died in 2005, we have all had to cope in our various ways, but mum has been a tower of strength, and the amount of work she has done to make today a success has just been phenomenal. I know dad would be very happy and proud of mum, and I just hoping he's looking down on us all now.'

## Fond farewells

'Last night, as I was putting the finishing touches to the dress and downing the final Valium in my bathroom cabinet, Mum came into my bedroom, put her arm around my shoulder and said: "Can I have one?"

'No, no, she didn't really say that, she said: "Tomorrow I'm going to lose a daughter and gain a bathroom". I didn't quite know how to take that.'

## Mother's wisdom

'Mum has always given me sensible advice which, as some of you will know, but hopefully will not talk about, I have not always followed.

'There was the night she said to me: "Never, in any circumstances, marry a man whose toenails are longer than your fingernails." Very sound advice, as decent sheets can be very expensive indeed.

'Then there was the evening when she told me for the first time about sex. It was the (*insert yesterday's date and wait for laughter*).

'And finally, the best advice of all: who ever you marry, make sure you mean it. And I do.'

## Wish you were here

'There are various people who cannot be here today and I'd like to say a few words about them if I may.

'Duncan Little, who was my best friend at University, is unfortunately stuck on the Isle of Mull watching small birds mate. He always was a bit funny like that.

'Lynne Black is in labour. I know this because she sent me a text five minutes before I went into the registry office – this is true, I promise you – saying, "I am in labour". I knew I should have switched off that bloody mobile.

'Finally, Clare Armstrong, who was my flatmate in Liverpool, is in Milwaukee... getting married, this very day. So although I am sad they can't be with us, at least they are all doing something enjoyable. If you count watching birds mate, going into labour and getting married as enjoyable.'

## Otherwise engaged

'I said that as part of my speech I would list all the friends who can't be with us today. This was so I didn't have to try to make jokes, which I'm very bad at.

'I'm very sad that my friend Georgina Tucker isn't here. She's in Hong Kong on a business trip. She said she'd bring me back some pak choi. Indira Hall is, sadly, not very well. Indira was my matron when I was training as a nurse in Preston and I'm very sad she can't be here.

'Tom's (*the groom*) friend Martin Wells couldn't be with us today. He sent us a message from Wormwood Scrubs, sorry, Sandhurst to say congratulations. We miss all of our absent friends and urge the rest of you to enjoy yourselves all the more in their place.'

## Family favourites

'One of the best things about getting married to Harry (*the groom*) is that it brings together my two favourite families in the whole world. Luckily, our two sets of parents get on very well together – better than Harry and me, in fact – and those of you who are married will know how much this means to a couple. There's some talk of them actually becoming a rowing four, but I think that might be just a rumour.'

## By any other name...

'I read in the *Times* recently that it's all the fashion nowadays to combine the surnames of the two families so that the wife does not have to give up her name.

'Perhaps this is why Brad and Angelina have become Brangelina. I suppose that's better than Jitt. That would mean my new surname is now (*insert combined surname*). Mind you, it doesn't always work. I have a friend called Emily West who has just married a man called Jerry Pankhurst so either they call themselves the Pests or...'

## Spread a little happiness

'A good friend of mine who's sceptical about these things asked me the other day what I was hoping for from marriage. What an odd question, I thought at first, as I took the tube back home. I was so engrossed in thinking about it that I got on a train going to West Ruislip instead of Ealing Broadway.

'But I thought and thought about it and eventually I came up with an answer. Actually I came up with lots of answers. I want to be happy, I want to have lots of children, I guess the things that most people would say. But actually my main hope is that I can make Garth (*the groom*) happy. Because if he's happy, I know I will be.'

## Changing for the better

'I know that from now on, everything will be very different, and I hope and trust — in fact, I *know* — it will be better as well.'

'I shall start getting to work on time, because Michael (*the groom*) will wake me up. I shan't faint with hunger at 9.55am because Michael will have cooked me a lovely English breakfast every day.'

'And when I get back home in the evening, Michael will have prepared me a perfumed bath and a glass of gin and tonic (not too much ice, Michael), which will be waiting for me on the side of the tub.

'And I'll be able to look out of the bathroom window and see the pigs flying off into the sky above our house.'

# Toasts given by the bride

Traditionally, the bride does not make a speech, so there is no formal toast for her to make. This means she can choose to toast whomever she likes. Popular choices are her parents/groom's parents and family, her bridesmaids/helpers, absent friends, particularly if one is a parent or close relative, and/or her new husband!

## Poetry in motion

'As I was searching for something to express what I wanted to say to Rob today, I came across a poem by another Rob, the poet Robert Browning, who wrote: "Grow old along with me! The best is yet to be." I want to thank Rob for agreeing to grow old with me and say that, after such a brilliant day, that if the best is yet to come, I can't wait! So please fill up your glasses and toast my new husband – to Robert!'

## Mum's the word

'There's an old Chinese saying that to find a good wife you must look for the daughter of a great mother. After what Mum and Dad have organized for me today, I think we'll all agree, this is one truly great mother. And Ed and I would like to ask you to make a special toast to thank her. To Mum!'

## Hard labour

'Many of you might have expected my sister Claire to be my
chief bridesmaid and, indeed, that was the original plan.
Unfortunately she can't be here today as she's virtually in
labour – now what kind of feeble excuse is that? Ladies and
gentlemen, please raise your glasses to Claire, the best sister
anyone could have.'

## Thanks, maids

'I'd like to take this opportunity to thank my lovely
bridesmaids for doing my make-up, doing my hair, arranging
my bouquet, helping me with my frock and, most importantly,
putting up with a complete maniac for the last six months.
I promise you, I'll leave you in peace now, girls. Let's drink to
them, ladies and gentlemen: The bridesmaids!'

# The chief
# bridesmaid's
## speech

# The chief bridesmaid

It's still a relatively new idea for the chief bridesmaid – or 'best woman' – to make a speech, but if the bride plans to speak it can be a nice touch if you do, too.

Your speech is pretty much a free zone, tradition-wise. You'll probably want to talk about your relationship with the bride, about her and the groom, perhaps adding some stories from the hen night or the wedding build-up.

**When to speak**

The chief bridesmaid will usually speak after the father of the bride, groom and bride, and before the best man, who is traditionally the last speaker.

What to say

- Compliment the bride and thank her for choosing you.
- Talk about the run-up to the wedding.
- Share some memories of your relationship with the bride.
- Compliment the ushers on behalf of the bridesmaids.
- Toast the bride and groom.

Alternatives

- You may prefer to make a joint speech with one of the ushers or even the best man.

# The basics

Although there is a growing trend for bridesmaids to make speeches, it is neither traditional nor compulsory and will not happen at all weddings – it is a matter of personal choice.

As chief bridesmaid or maid/matron of honour, you have fewer compulsory elements to include in your speech and the greater part of it can be about the bride, your relationship with her and her relationship with the groom.

**What to include in your speech**

Obviously the formality of your speech depends on the formality of the occasion, but if you are the bride's sister, or your relationship with her as a very old friend is well known, then you can get away with poking a bit more fun at her!

- Compliment the bride and thank her for choosing you as her chief bridesmaid.
- Comment on the preparations for the wedding – this is the time you have spent together, both in the run-up to the day and in the time directly before the ceremony.
- Share a memory of the bride that highlights an amusing or endearing part of her personality.
- Compliment the ushers on behalf of the bridesmaids.
- Toast the bride and groom.

# Sample speech snippets

### Sister act

'It feels like I've known Hattie (*the bride*) all my life. Actually, I *have* known Hattie all my life because for those of you who don't know, I'm her sister, and when I was born, Hattie had been in the world for a while already. Sibling loyalty means I'm not allowed to say exactly how many years, but it's a number between six and eight. And since I'm 24...

'So you can understand that when Brian (*the groom*) suggested that my speech contain some juicy anecdotes from Hattie's early life, I replied that the juicy bits had to start from her seventh birthday. He looked a bit disappointed, so I suspect he wanted some stories about how she used to cry and kick her legs about when she was having her nappy changed. Sorry, Brian – you'll have to get your kicks elsewhere.'

## Matchmaking

'It's a well-known fact that I introduced Phil (*the groom*) to Sue (*the bride*). In fact, I was living with Phil at the time. (*Pause.*) No, not like that. We were sharing a flat. And I saw immediately that they were made for each other.

'Phil never did the washing up while Sue is the neatest person on this earth. She actually enjoys washing up. Phil takes care of his personal appearance... so *little* that far from being the groom, he actually *needs* a groom – preferably one of those stable girls with big hairbrushes for the horse's mane.

'Sue fits the bill. She's still got an instrument for getting stones out of horse's hooves from when she had a pony. She'll need it with Phil.'

## Older and wiser

'Joanne (*the bride*) is as perfect an elder sister as you could wish for. She's kind, she's understanding, she always has plenty of cash on her. She has been a shoulder to cry on for me.

'I remember once coming home from being stood up yet again by some spotty sixth-former, and she explained at great length that men were all good-for-nothings (actually she used a different word from that) and we women should never, but never, go anywhere near them. Lucky for Tim (*the groom*) that she didn't take her own advice!'

## Ever-so-slightly fussy

'As you know, or perhaps if you come from Les's (*the groom*) side of the family, you don't know, Mary (*the bride*) has a bit of a reputation in our family for... um, how can I say this politely?... wanting everything to be just so.

'I did notice, for example, that the two little models of the bride and groom on top of the cake had been straightened up between the time I arrived here and the time we sat down for lunch. Now who could have done that?

'When we were choosing the dress – and I kid you not – we looked at 42 different wedding dress catalogues. 42! In the time it took Mary to choose the patterns for the bridesmaids' dresses, England could have won a World Cup. Well, perhaps not won it, but definitely reached the quarter-finals.'

## A shining example

'I know that as the chief bridesmaid, my job is to tell you lots of stories about Donna's (*the bride*) misspent youth hanging out with dodgy lads at funfairs, halls and so on... a kind of best woman's speech. But as you know, Donna didn't have a misspent youth and has never been near a dodgy bloke in her entire life.

'When she walks past a building site, the workers put their tops back *on*. She was always held up to the rest of us as the example we should follow. She always did her homework the same day it was set; she helped Mum and Dad with the washing up after every meal; she used to take the old lady who lived next door's dog for a walk.

'That is the kind of woman Donna is – helpful and good with animals. Perfect preparation for marriage.'

## Wild youth

'In fact, I know from stories passed down by aged aunts and grannies that Charlotte's seventh birthday was a bit of an event. Actually, "trauma" was the word used by Mum.

'She hired the Old Kitchen in Kenwood House for Charlotte's birthday party, and invited Charlotte's class. And they ran amok. The damage ran to thousands of pounds, apparently. Even now, if you go to Kenwood House, there's a sign on the door saying "no hawkers, no free papers, no friends of Charlotte Jones".

'I'm not going to say Charlotte was a centre of chaos, disruption and general mayhem, because we all know that already. What I am going to say is that despite all that, she is the most high-spirited, loving, charming girl you could imagine. And she still is.'

## It started with a bang

'Keira (*the bride*) and Jon (*the groom*) have been going out for nearly four years now. I was actually present the night they met. We were standing in the kitchen swigging back the Chardonnay, when Keira grabbed me by the sleeve and said: "Who's that incredibly dishy bloke who's just walked in?" And I remember, I replied, "You mean the one with Jon?"

'Keira told me later that their relationship had started with a bang. She meant it literally, as their first date had been a fireworks night at Jon's school. And if you think I'm going to put in jokes about lighting the blue touch paper or stoking the bonfire... I'm afraid you're absolutely right.'

## Games people play

'I remember Carla (*the bride*) used to play a particularly sadistic game with me when I was about six and she was ten. It was called, "All at once or one at a time?"

'She would get a pack of playing cards and ask me, "All at once or one at a time?" and if I replied "all at once" she would throw the whole pack of cards in the air so they went all over the living room, and I would have to pick them all up as quickly as I could.

'If I said "one at a time" – you've guessed it – she would throw the cards one at a time all over the room, and I would have to *run around* picking them all up. And if I didn't, she beat me up.

'So I was a bit worried today when she came up to me just before the meal with a big pile of napkins and said "All at once or one at a time?"'

## The ultimate wedding planner

'Kathy (*the bride*) is just so well organized that she puts the rest of us to shame. The hotel manager just told me he lost the booking for the reception because they didn't keep bookings made more than five years ago!

'I thought you might like to see the instructions that Kathy gave me about how the bouquet should be (*bring out computer print-out that falls concertina-like from your hands to the floor, it's so long*). The colours of the flowers come from one of those paint-mixing machines.

'We had to make three trips to the shop to get the blue right. And I didn't even get to catch the bouquet!'

## Sporty type

'Lots of men have been put off Yolanda (*the bride*) by her sporty prowess. I was jogging with her in Alexandra Park once and I heard a man mutter to his friend, "Blimey! It's Serena Williams!" Of course he may have been talking about me...

'Everybody knows that Yolanda was the Middlesex area champion in the 100 metres for three years running. So her beautiful long legs have had two opposite functions – one to attract the men, and the other to run away from them. But finally a man has been able to run fast enough to catch up! But my suspicion is that this time she was running deliberately slowly...'

# Standing in

# The stand-in speaker

Standing in for the father of the bride or the best man can be a tricky job. If you're lucky, you will have been warned in plenty of time, but if you're a last-minute substitute, don't worry, there is still time to prepare an excellent speech.

The family may prefer a close friend to speak rather than a parent, or perhaps you are a step-parent. Maybe the best man has pulled out at the last minute. Whatever the reason, if you are the person standing in and making a speech, then this is the chapter for you.

## The basics

The key speeches at any wedding might not always be given by the obvious first choice. The father of the bride, for instance, may be estranged from his daughter's family or he may have died before her wedding. Likewise, an illness or accident may deprive the reception of its best man or chief bridesmaid.

In these and many other circumstances, the families of the bride and groom may need to find a replacement speaker. As the wedding day approaches, they will start to look around among friends and family for suitable stand-ins. And this is when you may find yourself asked to give a speech on behalf of someone else. Here's what you need to know and do to survive the experience.

### What to include in your speech
So, what is expected of a stand-in speaker?

- Introduce yourself and explain briefly your relationship to the bride (and groom).
- If one of the bride or groom's parents has passed away, you should honour them in your speech. See pages 142–143 for ideas on how to do this.
- Thank the guests for joining the celebrations.
- Thank all those who have paid for any part of the wedding and helped to organize the day.
- Compliment the bride.
- Welcome the groom.
- Propose a toast to the bride and groom.

# Useful phrases

If you have been asked to give the first speech, you will probably have known the bride for a number of years, but still take the time to speak to her family beforehand, especially her mother, who traditionally plays a silent role on the day. The following are a few options to cut and paste into your own speech.

## The introduction

- I am delighted to be here and feel very privileged to have been Nicola's stepfather for the last 15 years.
- I feel very honoured to stand here and speak on behalf of my father, who would have loved to see my sister Nicola marry John.
- As Nicola's godfather, I've been asked by her parents to welcome you all to her wedding and say a few words about their beautiful daughter.

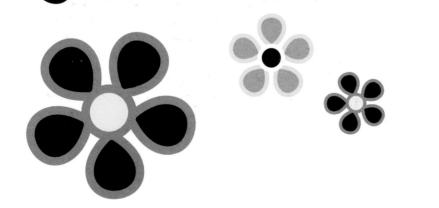

## 2  The thanks

- Ladies and gentlemen, I'd like to thank you all for being here today to witness the marriage of Nicola and John.
- Ladies and gentlemen, I'm delighted to see so many of you here today to share this special day with Nicola and John.
- Ladies and gentlemen, I know how delighted Nicola and John are to see so many of their friends and relatives on *their special day/the most important day of their lives.*

## 3  Thanking contributors

- Today would not have been possible without the generous help of both sets of parents, Ken and Angela, and Fred and Jane, and I know that the couple are very grateful to them.
- Nicola and John have done a wonderful job with the wedding arrangements, but they would like to make a special mention of Vikki, who very generously donated the magnificent flowers.

## 4  Compliment the bride

Here, we have given you a few options to cut and paste into your own speech:

- I know that Ken and Angela are very proud of their daughter Nicola. She has worked extremely hard to get where she is today (*name her career or mention what she studied at university*) and she is a *beautiful/radiant/gorgeous* bride. However, I will always remember her as a *scruffy/an inquisitive/a mischievous baby/child/adolescent*.

- Nicola makes a *glamorous/radiant/gorgeous/lovely* bride but, to me, she will always be a *scruffy/mischievous/solemn/beautiful baby/child/teenager*. Her family and friends are so proud of her, not only because she has been so successful in (*name her career/studying/hobbies or achievements*), but because she is as *beautiful on the inside as she is on the outside/a generous, warm-hearted and loving woman*.

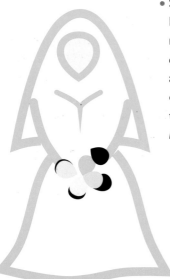

- Seeing Nicola here today, looking so *beautiful/radiant/happy*, I would never recognize the *baby/child/teenager* who loved nothing better than to (*tell a sweet anecdote, e.g., play with caterpillars/climb trees/play weddings with her dolls, etc*). I am *honoured/proud* to be here today speaking on behalf of her family, and I know that Ken and Angela are so proud that she has grown into such a *wonderful/sweet-natured/kind* woman.

## 5  Welcome the groom

- I am not only delighted for Nicola on her wedding day, but also for John. He is a good man and I know that Ken and Angela are delighted to welcome him into their family. Nicola and John make a beautiful couple and they have a lot in common. I am sure that they will be as happy in 20 years' time as they are today.
- John, you are the perfect man for Nicola. You are kind, warm-hearted and generous, and she deserves nothing less. On behalf of Ken and Angela, I am delighted to welcome you into the family.
- I've always thought that it would be difficult for Nicola to find a man who was worthy of her, but I was wrong. John is perfect for her, and I know that I speak on Ken and Angela's behalf when I say how delighted we all are that you have married Nicola.

## 6  Toast the bride and groom

Wait for all of the glasses to be filled before asking guests to stand for the first toast. Remember to wait for silence before starting the toast, as you don't want to be drowned out by scraping chairs.

- Ladies and gentlemen, please be upstanding and raise your glasses. I give you... the bride and groom.
- Ladies and gentlemen, please be upstanding and charge your glasses. I give you... the bride and groom.
- Ladies and gentlemen, please be upstanding and join me in a toast to... the bride and groom.

# Sample speech snippets

## Dad would be so proud

'It gives me great pleasure and, of course, a certain amount of sadness, to be making this speech. As many of you will know, Rosalyn's (*the bride*) father Jack died just over three years ago, and Millie, Rosalyn's mother, asked me to give Rosalyn away today.

'I've known the family for many years, and I was a friend of Jack's both at University, and afterwards when we belonged to the same cricket club. I know that Jack would be tremendously proud of his beautiful daughter on her wedding day, and I am very honoured to be here to represent him.'

## Second best man

'If you were expecting Phil (*the original best man*) to be standing up in front of you today, you may be a little surprised to see me!

'I feel a bit like the singer who was asked to substitute Pavarotti at the last second. Everyone will be pleased and grateful to see you, but it wasn't what they paid for.

'So if you want a refund, please see Oliver (*the groom*) as you go out.'

## Sorry he couldn't be here...

'There's a statistic that you see every so often doing the rounds of the Internet about what are the ten most stressful things you can do in your life. And apparently number one – yes, number one – is speaking in public.

'Well, as you've probably noticed, this stress has got to Terry's (*the groom*) brother Ed, and he was rushed off to the National Hospital for Nervous Diseases this morning, still clutching his best man's speech in his right hand and mumbling "Ladies and gentlemen, please be upstanding, ladies and gentlemen, please be upstanding..."

'Actually, of course, Ed was not able to be here because of... (give real reason).'

## Quids in

'I've known Donald (*the groom*) for quite a long time now, and though I can't claim the kind of inside knowledge that his brother would have provided – ie no dirt, gossip, scandal, rude stories about losing his underwear on the London Underground, etc – I can tell you that Don is quite one of the kindest, most cheerful and intelligent men I have ever met. And that Hannah is very lucky to be marrying him.

'And Don, please make the cheque payable to...'

## She's lovely (it says here)

'I'm sure you'll agree that the most beautiful person in our company today is Sharon (*the bride*). Now I only met Sharon for the first time about 20 minutes ago, but I saw straightaway why... um... (*consult notes*) Billy! (*the groom*) would want to marry her. If she is as intelligent, kind and sympathetic as she is beautiful, then can I please marry her, too?

'In fact, of course, I've known Sharon and Bill for many years, and although I wasn't first choice for best man – not that I'm bitter or anything, oh no – I am honoured to be standing here to toast them.'

## Two great dynasties united

'In fact, though I am but a lowly latecomer to this table, I know both the families well. And by uniting the Johnsons and the Fielders, I feel that Alex and Megan (*the bride and groom*) are bringing together two families of integrity and also of great hospitality.

'In the case of the Johnsons – as I know to my cost – this hospitality can lead to hangovers of stupendous proportions. Even now, eight years later, I still don't know what happened to my socks at Alex's 21st birthday party'.

## Quote... unquote

'I've been told that it's a good idea to use quotations in wedding speeches, so I consulted various websites about which quotations to use in a wedding speech. As I am but a humble substitute, I fed in the word "substitute"... obviously I got The Who lyric, "I look quite tall but my heels are high" – but that didn't really seem appropriate, I felt, as I am wearing perfectly normal shoes.

'But after literally minutes of searching I got our old and reliable friend Bill Shakespeare – "a substitute shines brightly as a king". Well, it's my speech.'

## A substitute by any other name

'I looked up substitute in the Thesaurus and this is what I got: bogus, counterfeit, ersatz, fabricated, factitious, faked, false, falsie, hyped up, man-made, manufactured, mock, phony, plastic, queer, sham, simulated, specious, spurious, synthetic, unnatural, unreal – which cheered me up no end.'

# Civil
# partnerships

# The introduction of civil partnerships

Civil Partnerships (CPs) give gay and lesbian couples the same legal rights as a married couple. Previously, only 'commitment ceremonies' existed, and these didn't give gay couples the same rights as a married couple.

Only same-sex couples can enter into a civil partnership. They were introduced in the UK in December 2005 and, though not technically weddings, are often called weddings by the gay couples who have them. After all, the civil partnership ceremony has the same function as a wedding, in that it celebrates the union of two people who have chosen to devote their lives to each other.

## Civil partnerships around the world

- More than 20 countries have introduced civil partnerships, including some states of the US. Other countries are currently debating their introduction.
- The first country to recognize same-sex unions was Denmark in 1989. The Danish for civil partnership is *registreret partnerskab*.
- In many European countries, civil partnership is called PACS (*pacte civile de solidarité* in French) which has led to new expressions and verbs being coined, for example, *se pacser*.
- In France, one in ten PACS has been dissolved.
- In the UK, the civil partner of a peer or knight is not entitled to the same courtesy title that a wife would be.
- The most famous civil partnership in the UK was between singer Elton John and David Furnish on 21 December 2005.

## Making a speech at a civil partnership

If you are asked to make a speech at a civil partnership ceremony, you do not need to worry that your speech should be 'special' in some way. After all, the feelings and spirit of the occasion are just the same as for any wedding.

At a conventional wedding, the roles of the speakers has been carved out by tradition and practice over many years. It may be that in future the kinds of speeches made at a gay wedding will change and the participants take on different roles, too. However, in these early days, it is fine simply to adapt the speeches that have traditionally been made at opposite-sex weddings. We've given you some suggestions for these below.

Whether you are speaking at your own or someone else's ceremony, the key principles of making the speech remain the same – to celebrate with warmth and affection the union of two people who are dear to the people present.

**What to include in your speech**
- Thank everyone involved in organizing the day.
- Welcome and thank guests.
- Mention friends/family.
- Include some affectionate and humorous stories about the participants.
- Stay clear of certain areas (see pages 26–29).
- Don't speak for too long.

# Sample speech snippets

### The long and winding road...

'It is very heartening and pleasing to see so many of our friends and family at the ceremony today. It has been a long and occasionally difficult road to get to this point, but we have always been supported in every way by our friends and family, and Joe (*the partner of the speaker*) and I would like to thank everybody who has sent messages of support, or who have helped us in all kinds of small but significant ways.'

## How we met

'As many of you will know, I first met Gill (*the partner of the speaker*) when we were both working at an events management company in London. On my first day, I walked into the reception area and Gill, who had already been working there for several months, welcomed me as if I were a long lost friend. So it's really a case of from one reception to another!'

## They're the perfect couple

'Those of us who have been in Lisa and Fiona's (*the couple*)
group of friends over the last few years, will know that they
have always seemed to us to be the epitome of a stable,
loving couple.'

## Straight up

'As a straight man asked to be best man at a gay wedding, I
feel a mixture of emotions. Of course I feel a bit like the
proverbial spare part, though I notice that as usual with gay
men, Paul and Larry (*the couple*) have surrounded themselves
with gorgeous women... But also I feel honoured that they
should have asked me to help celebrate their union. But why
did they pick me? Well, someone had to be the worst-
dressed person here...'

## A time to celebrate

'A lot of people have asked Phil (*the partner of the speaker*)
and me why we decided to enter into a civil partnership. I
think the main reason, at least from my point of view, was
to affirm what was important for me about our
relationship: my love, devotion and commitment to Phil, and
to show to the world this commitment, and to allow other
people – in fact, all of you gathered here today – to
celebrate it.'

## Say it in song

'There's a website, which naturally I consulted before writing my speech, which lists the top gay songs of all time. This is apparently known as the Homo Hundred. I had a quick look through it to see if there were any appropriate titles. Some of them were only marginally so: for example, *Better the devil you know* by Kylie, or *So many men, so little time* by Miquel Brown.

'Some were definitely not right, like *I want to break free* by Queen. But for the most part, they were delightfully suitable for today's celebration. *I'm so excited* by the Pointer Sisters, which summed up exactly how I felt, and I'm sure everybody felt, when we woke up this morning.

'*This is my life* by Shirley Bassey was at number 100, which I'm sure anybody who has been to a wedding of any kind has felt at some point during the day. *Mad about the boy* was at number 8, and I don't need to add anything to that.

'And of course, at no.1, what else could it be but *I feel love* by Donna Summer? Perfect.'

## Rights and rewards

'Kay and Viv have been a strong, faithful couple for as long as I have known them, and today is a powerful and, for me, moving demonstration of their love and commitment. As many of you will know, both Kay and Viv have been tireless workers for gay rights over the years, and it is so right and appropriate that they have come together like this today.'

## A new son

'Let me say first of all how proud and pleased that Margery (*wife of speaker and mother of one of the couple*) and I are to be here today, and to welcome Gerry (*partner of the speaker's son*) into our family. We have always regarded Gerry as a sort of second son, and now he actually is one! We have known Gerry for about ten years and we're sure that Pete (*son*) and he will be very happy together.'

## Map-reading skills

'We are very lucky that Helen and Joanna actually made it here today. Everybody knows that Helen has the time-keeping capacity of a Peruvian goatherd, and Joanna the map-reading ability of a... I was going to say a man, but of course men are good at map-reading. I remember driving Joanna home once – we had to get from Kensal Rise to Camden, and she was giving me directions. It was only when we went past Cardiff Arms Park (*pause*)... for the second time... that she realized we might have been lost.'

# Index

**a**bsent friends and relatives 11, 54, 123, 141, 146, 147
anecdotes 13, 14, 18, 48

**b**est man
  role of 98
  thanked by groom 11, 80, 84–5
best man's speech
  alternative speech 99
  the basics 100–103
  about the groom 101–2, 106–7
  compliment the bride 103, 107
  the final toast 103
  telegrams 103
  the thanks 99, 101
  who are you? 101
  brief outline of speech 11
  do's and don'ts 104–5
  and order of speakers 10
  sample speech snippets 106–111
  toasts 103, 112–13
  what to say 99
  when to speak 99
body language 40
breathing 39
bride
  best man's comments on 11, 16, 83
  compliments to 10, 11, 24, 79, 80, 82–3, 107, 131, 141, 144, 148
  thanked by groom 84
  toasts to 10, 11, 54, 55, 59, 60, 65, 74–5, 94, 95, 99, 103, 112–13, 130, 131, 141, 145
bride's father
  brief outline of speech 10
  and order of speakers 10
bride's father: thanked by groom 80, 81

bride's father's speech 58–75
  alternative speech 59
  the basics 60–65
  the bride 62
  general chat 64–5
  the thanks 61
  the toast 65
  the welcome 61
  welcome the groom 63
  sample speech snippets 66–73
  toasts by 65, 74–5
  what to say 59, 60
  when you speak 59
bride's mother 98
  gifts to 54, 80
  thanks to 118, 119, 121
  toast to 126
bride's parents
  thanks to 11, 80, 82, 95, 143
  toast to 94, 95
bride's speech 79, 116–27
  alternative speech 117
  the basics 118–19
  brief outline of speech 11
  and order of speakers 10
  what to say 117
  when to speak 117
bridesmaids
  gifts to 54
  thanks to 11, 85, 94, 118, 119, 127
  toast to 11, 55, 79, 80, 85, 94, 99, 127
  see also chief bridesmaid

**c**ardinal rules 12–13
cardinal sins 14–15
chief bridesmaid's speech 98, 130–37
  alternative speech 130

  the basics 131
  brief outline of speech 11
  and order of speakers 10
  sample speech snippets 132–6
  what to say 130
  when to speak 130
civil partnerships 152–7
  making a speech 153
  sample speech snippets 154–7
cue cards 36, 43

**d**rinking 35, 43

**e**ye contact 38

**f**amily friend's speech see stand-in speaker
friends: as sources of stories 18, 42

**g**ames 32–3
gay partnerships 152–7
gifts
  guests thanked for their gifts 11, 80, 82, 117, 119
  presentation during a toast 54
godfathers 59, 142
good delivery 34–35, 43
groom
  best man's comments on 11, 16, 101–2, 106–7, 111
  compliments to 11, 147
  toasts to 11, 54, 55, 59, 60, 65, 74–5, 99, 103, 112–13, 130, 131, 141, 145
  welcomed 63, 141, 145
groom's mother, gifts to 54, 80
groom's parents, thanks to 11, 61, 80, 143

groom's speech 78–95
  alternative speech 79
  the basics 80–85
  thank the best man 84–5
  thank your bride 84
  thank and toast the bridesmaids 85
  thank your new father-in-law 81
  thank your guests 82
  thank your in-laws 82
  brief outline of speech 11
  and order of speakers 10
  sample speech snippets 86–93
  toasts by 85, 94–5
  what is expected of the groom? 80
  what to say 79
  when to speak 79
guests
  thanked for their attendance 10, 11, 59, 60, 61, 80, 82, 119, 141
  thanked for their gifts 11, 80, 82, 117, 119
  toast to 118, 119

humour 12

joint speech 16, 59, 79, 99, 111, 117, 130
jokes 22, 38, 39, 50–51
  in-jokes 29

key game 33

limerick game 32

maid/matron of honour 131
master of ceremonies 10
messages 11, 54, 99

one-liners 47–8
order of speakers 10, 25

photographs 18, 19, 59

positive thinking 40–41, 43
preparation 13
  break down each element 16
  decide on what kind of speech to make 16
  preparing your speech 16
  speech-making aids 17
prompts
  cue cards 36, 43
  memory joggers 36
  what the experts say 37
props 16, 17, 30–31, 42, 99

quotations 13

rehearsing speech 13, 17, 25, 34, 42, 43
research 18–23, 42
  comparing bride/groom to a celebrity 21
  friends as sources of stories 18
  get some help 23
  hobbies and interests 22
  jokes 22
  the meaning of names 23
  newspaper cuttings 20
  old photographs 18, 19
  school reports 23
  working life 22
  Zodiac signs 20–21
right material
  quick speech checklist 25
  tailored to fit 25
  tips for success 24

singing game 32
slides 16
speech structure 46–53
  end on a high 52–3
  good beginnings 46–8
  meaty middles 49–52
stage fright 41

stand-in speaker 140–49
  the basics 140–41
  compliment the bride 144
  thanking contributors 143
  the introduction 142
  the thanks 143
  toast the bride and groom 145
  welcome the groom 145
  brief outline of speech 10
  and order of speakers 10
  sample speech snippets 146–9
stepfathers 59, 142
stunts 16, 99
subject matter do's and don'ts 26–9
success, ten steps to 38–41
sweepstake game 33

telegrams 98, 103, 104
  invented funny 16, 99
timing 13, 25, 39, 43
toastmaster 10, 98
toasts 41, 43
  absent friends 54
  by bride's father 65, 74–5
  classic best man's toasts 112–13
  do's and don'ts of toast-making 55
  purpose of 54
  see also under individuals
tone 12

ushers, compliments to 11, 130, 131

videos, home 16, 31, 59, 99

wedding costs 65
  contributors to costs thanked 10, 60
wedding speech checklist
  the big day 43
  the build-up 42
  once you've agreed to speak 42
  only a week to go 43

# About confetti.co.uk

Confetti.co.uk, founded in 1999, is the leading destination for brides- and grooms-to-be. Every month over 700,00 people visit www.confetti.co.uk to help them plan their weddings and special occasions. Here is a quick guide to our website

**Weddings** The wedding channel is packed full of advice and ideas to make your day more special and your planning less stressful. Our personalized planning tools will ensure you won't forget a thing.

**Celebrations** Checklists, advice and ideas for every party and celebration.

**Fashion and beauty** View hundreds of wedding, bridesmaid and party dresses and accessories. Get expert advice on how to look and feel good.

**Travel** Search for the most idyllic destinations for your honeymoon, wedding abroad or romantic breaks. Get fun ideas for hen and stag weekends.

**Suppliers** Thousands of suppliers to choose from including venues, gift lists companies, cake makers, florists and bridal retailers.

**Café** Talk to other brides and grooms and get ideas from our real life weddings section. Ask Aunt Betti, our agony aunt, for advice.

**Shop** All your wedding and party essentials in one place. The ranges include planning essentials, books and CDs, personalised stationery for weddings and celebrations, create your own trims, ribbons and papers, table decorations, party products including hen and stag, memories and gifts. If you'd like to do your shopping in person or view all the ranges before buying online, please visit the confetti stores.

## Online

- Shop online 24 hours a day 7 days a week, use quick searches by department, product code or keyword, use the online order tracking facility and view brand new products as soon as they come out.
- Shop by phone on 0870 840 6060 Monday to Friday between 9 am and 5 pm.
- Shop by post by sending a completed order form to Confetti, Freepost NEA9292, Carr Lane, Low Moor, Bradford, BD12 0BR or fax on 01274 805 741.

## By phone/freepost

Request your free copy of our catalogue online at www.confetti.co.uk or call 0870 840 6060

## In store

**London** – 80 Tottenham Court Road, London, W1T 4TE

**Leeds** – The Light, The Headrow, Leeds, LS1 8TL

**Birmingham** – 43 Temple Street, Birmingham B2 5DP

**Glasgow** – 15–17 Queen Street, Glasgow, G1 3ED

**Reading** – 159 Friar Street, Reading, RG1 1HE

Executive Editor **Katy Denny**
Managing Editor **Clare Churly**
Executive Art Editor **Penny Stock**
Design **Cobalt id**
Production Manager **Ian Paton**